LIVERPOOL HEROES

Book 3

17 Liverpool holders of the Victoria Cross

Edited by Ann Clayton

Researched by
Sid Lindsay
Bill Sergeant and
Ann Clayton

**NOEL CHAVASSE VC
MEMORIAL
ASSOCIATION**
2009

First published in Great Britain in 2009 by the

NOEL CHAVASSE VC MEMORIAL ASSOCIATION
Registered Charity No. 1112413

Copyright NCVCMA 2009
ISBN 978-0-9553495-2-2

All proceeds from the sale of this book will go towards the maintenance of the
Victoria Cross Memorial Statue in the City of Liverpool

Further copies, price £7.00 + p&p may be obtained from:

DONALD ALLERSTON,
12 WEXFORD AVENUE,
HALE VILLAGE,
MERSEYSIDE L24 5RY
UNITED KINGDOM

Printed by Printstat, St. Helens, Merseyside WA10 2PF UK

Contents

Foreword   5

1.   Philip Eric BENT, VC, DSO   7
2.   Charles George BONNER, VC, DSC   11
3.   Christopher BUSHELL, VC, DSO   15
4.   Walter Norris CONGREVE, VC, KCB, MVO   19
5.   William La Touche CONGREVE, VC, DSO, MC   25
6.   Edgar Christopher COOKSON, VC, DSO   33
7.   Jack Thomas COUNTER, VC   37
8.   John Thomas DAVIES, VC   41
9.   Charles Calveley FOSS, VC, CB, DSO   45
10. Ian Edward FRASER, VC, DSC   49
11. George Ward GUNN, VC, MC   59
12. Harry HAMPTON, VC   65
13. Henry James KNIGHT, VC   69
14. John Simpson KNOX, VC   73
15. Andrew MOYNIHAN, VC   79
16. John O'NEILL, VC, MM   87
17. Edward UNWIN, VC, CB, CMG   91

Addenda   97

Appendix I: Introduction to Book 1 by Sid Lindsay   103

Appendix II: The Memorial   109

$\mathscr{F}$oreword
by
Bill Sergeant

I am chairman of the Noel Chavasse VC Memorial Association (NCVCMA), a charity established to commission, fund and erect a memorial statue in Liverpool to the memory of Chavasse VC & Bar, MC and fifteen other recipients of the Victoria Cross who were born here in the City. The stories of these sixteen brave men are told in *Liverpool Heroes - Book 1*, copies of which are still available. In the first book I outlined the origins and objectives of NCVCMA, and the sculptor commissioned to produce the memorial, Tom Murphy, explained the thought processes behind his design (reprinted in this book as **Appendix II**).

This is the third volume in our series of books about recipients of the nation's highest award for valour, the Victoria Cross. Book 1 dealt with Noel Chavasse VC & Bar MC and fifteen others, born in Liverpool, who were awarded this honour between 1857 and 1918; Book 2 told the stories of another eighteen Victoria Cross winners who were closely connected with this great city. I realised from the outset that to do justice to the mass of research which the late Sid Lindsay had carried out, we would need another two or three volumes. Although some of the men covered in this and the soon-to-be-published fourth volume have more tenuous connections with Liverpool, I have decided to retain the series name of *Liverpool Heroes*.

The introductory notes which Sid Lindsay wrote himself are reproduced in full as Appendix I on page 103; Sid's huge contribution to the telling of the stories of these brave men is most gratefully acknowledged by the Association. Sid, in his turn, would have wished to acknowledge the efforts of the Noel Chavasse VC Memorial Association in having his research published, especially as the proceeds from the first two books made a significant contribution to our project to erect a fitting memorial to Chavasse and our Liverpool Heroes. I am pleased and proud to say that after almost three years we finally managed to raise the necessary funds, and on 17 August 2008 our memorial statue was unveiled. It now stands proudly in Abercromby Square, close to the house where the Chavasse family lived while Noel's father was Bishop of Liverpool. Perhaps I can be forgiven for any bias when I say that Tom Murphy, our sculptor, has produced a wonderful bronze statue which will ensure that these brave men are remembered for many, many years to come. The happy occasion of the unveiling was clouded by the death of Lieutenant Commander Ian Fraser VC, the last surviving Royal Naval holder of the award and a man who lived for almost his whole life here on Merseyside, in Wallasey. Ian was due to perform the actual unveiling ceremony but was too ill to attend and died shortly afterwards. The unveiling was actually performed by Tom Chavasse, nephew of Noel, and Noel's great nephew, Charles Chavasse. Photographs of the Memorial may be found at the end of this book.

Sadly, one of the founder members of the Noel Chavasse VC Memorial Association, George Poynton, also passed away before he could see the fruits of our labours. I would like to dedicate this volume to the memory of these two men, each of whom in his own way has left behind a valuable legacy here on Merseyside.

Bill Sergeant, Chairman,

Noel Chavasse VC Memorial Association

May 2009

$\mathcal{P}$hilip Eric Bent VC DSO

Philip Eric Bent VC DSO

P hilip Bent was born on 3 January 1891 in Halifax, Nova Scotia, the son of Sophie and Frank Piers Bent, about whom little is known other than that they were still living in Halifax in 1901. While still just a boy, he came to England with his mother and was educated at the Grammar School in Ashby-de-la-Zouche (now Ashby School), Leicestershire. He left school in 1907 to join HMS *Conway*, the training ship in the River Mersey, where as well as proving himself a satisfactory sailor he also gained a reputation as a boxer, a sport held in high regard on the ship. It is his service on board HMS *Conway* which brings Bent within the scope of this book.

Philip was a Senior Cadet Captain in his final term, leaving *Conway* in December 1910 to become an apprentice on the *Vimeria*, a steel four-masted barque of some 2,200 tons. Built by Charles Connell & Co of Glasgow in 1891, the year of Bent's birth, she was owned by John Hardie and Company of Glasgow, whose most famous vessel was the *Archibald Russell* and whose fleet consisted of six sailing ships and two steamers.

Bent was granted his Second Mate's Ticket in the early part of 1914 and in August found himself ashore when war was declared. He immediately enlisted with a friend, both believing that the war would be over by Christmas and they 'would have a bit of fun', as a private in 'A' Company, 1st Battalion, Royal Scots (City of Edinburgh) Regiment, at Edinburgh Castle. (Some say that Bent attended Edinburgh University and joined the University Battalion on the outbreak of war, but as yet there is no documentary evidence of this.) On 2 October 1914, he was granted a temporary commission as a Second Lieutenant in the newly formed 7th Battalion The Leicestershire Regiment at Aldershot. He was promoted Lieutenant in June 1915 and then transferred to the 9th Battalion which sailed for France in August that year. In April 1916 he was promoted to Temporary Captain, and this rank was substantiated when he was transferred to the Bedfordshire Regiment. Later in 1916, he was wounded in the neck, but resumed his duties after ten days in Base Hospital. He was gazetted Major in December 1916, and returned to the Leicestershire Regiment as second-in-command only to find that he was to be Temporary Lieutenant Colonel commanding the Battalion and at 23 years of age he was one of the youngest to ever hold that rank. The Commanding Officer, Lieutenant Colonel C.H. Haig had been wounded in the battle for Morval on 25 September 1916.

Bent was created a Companion of the Distinguished Service Order on 1 June 1917, and since landing in France in 1915 had never been very far from the action, having led his men from the front at Arras and elsewhere.

On the morning of 1 October 1917, the battle of Polygon Wood, part of General Haig's campaign to break out of the infamous Ypres Salient, had been raging for five days. The battle witnessed some of the bloodiest fighting of the war. Approximately seven kilometers due east of the town of Ypres and two kilometers south of the village of Zonnebeke, Polygon Wood at 0500 hrs that morning was subjected to a hurricane German artillery bombardment over a mile-long front from Reutelbeck northwards to Polygon Wood. The bombardment smothered the whole area with shells back to a thousand yards, and at 0530 hrs the German infantry appeared in strength and the 9th Leicestershires, who were at that time covering the 110th Brigade, were forced to give ground.

The situation quickly became critical owing to the confusion caused by this huge enemy attack and the intense artillery barrage. Philip Bent personally collected a platoon that was in reserve, and together with other companies and various regimental details, organised and led them forward on the counter-attack, after issuing orders to other officers as to the further defence of the line. The counter-attack was successful, and the enemy was checked. Positions which were to prove essentially important for subsequent operations were regained. The coolness and magnificent example shown to all ranks was exemplified by Philip Bent personally leading the charge with the cry of 'Come on the Tigers', (a reference to the Regimental cap badge). Sadly he was killed as he gave orders for re-consolidation as they gained their objective.

One of his fellow officers, in a letter to Philip's mother, Sophie, said :

> *It was the finest act possible and undoubtedly saved the day ... We feel the loss of our Colonel more than words can say, for he was beloved by all ranks. I am very proud to have had the privilege of knowing such a fine Christian gentleman, whose memory will live for ever in the history of the regiment.*

For his most conspicuous bravery in this action, Philip Bent was awarded the Victoria Cross. The investiture was held at Buckingham Palace on 2 March 1918, when his mother, Mrs. Sophie Bent, received from the King not only her son's Victoria Cross but also the Distinguished Service Order he had earned in June of 1917. Her son's other medals were sent to her in 1922, when she was living at 26b South Terrace, Littlehampton, Sussex. In 1923, his mother presented his medals to his old school at Ashby-de-la-Zouche, which in 1970 passed them for safe keeping to the Regimental Museum at Leicester. His portrait hangs in the Army Museum, Halifax, Nova Scotia, together with his Cadet Captain's badge and a silver medal he had won for boxing while on the *Conway*. His sword used to hang in the Parish Church of St. Helen at Ashby-de-la-Zouche. A memorial plaque was unveiled at Ashby School (the successor to Bent's old school) in 2005 and a replica of his Victoria Cross is displayed with it.

His mother was living in Hindhead, Surrey, when the war memorial was erected next to St. Alban's Church, Hindhead, and her son's name appears first on the memorial. Edward Unwin VC, another old Conway boy, spent his retirement years in Hindhead (see page 91 in this book).

Bent won his VC at Polygon Wood in what was a preliminary foray to the attack on Passchendaele between 26 October and 6 November 1917, an action which was described by Winston Churchill as a 'forlorn expenditure of valour and life without equal in futility'. During that action the Canadians suffered 16,000 casualties out of a strength of 20,000. Their Commanding Officer, Lieutenant General Sir Arthur Currie, tried to have the attack called off but was overruled by Haig. The magazine of the Canadian British Legion comments that Currie 'recommended the assault be called off because the battlefield was a quagmire, a mass of shell holes filled with suffocating yellow ooze that made it impossible to advance... He was convinced an assault would be suicidal'. Events proved his judgment to be correct, but in the assault the Canadians earned no less than nine VCs, including that of Hugh McDonald McKenzie (see *Liverpool Heroes* Book 1).

The tragic irony of Philip Bent's life is that if he had followed his sea career and stayed with the *Vimeria* he would probably have survived to live a long and happy life, for the sailing ship was still in service in 1925. In fact, had he let it be known when he enlisted that he held a Second Mate's ticket, the likelihood is that he would have found himself in the Royal Navy.

Bent has no known grave and his name is carved with pride on the great Tyne Cot Memorial, in Passchendaele, Belgium. Tyne Cot commemorates the 34,888 soldiers who fell in the Ypres Salient between August 1917 and the Armistice who have no known graves, and includes the names of two other VC winners, Corporal William Clamp, killed at Poelcapelle in October 1917, and Lance Corporal Ernest Seaman, killed at Terhand on 29 September 1917. Captain Clarence Jeffries VC, Sergeant Lewis McGee VC and Private James Robertson VC MM are amongst the 11,908 servicemen actually buried in Tyne Cot cemetery. It is indeed very satisfying to think that this great and solemn monument and its counterparts across the fields of France and Flanders will ensure that Philip Eric Bent and his comrades will never be forgotten.

In November 2004, the Chairman of Governors at Ashby School unveiled a framed replica Victoria Cross and a copy of Bent's citation in School House to ensure that future pupils are constantly reminded of this brave man. A second memorial was to be provided in memory of the school's other Victoria Cross winner, Lieutenant Colonel Bernard William Vann.

Charles George Bonner
VC DSC

Charles George Bonner VC DSC

Charles George 'Gus' Bonner was born on 29 December 1884, at Shuttington, in Warwickshire, the youngest son of Samuel Bonner JP, and of Jane, who was the daughter of Charles Hellaby of Bramcote Hall, Warwickshire. His father was a farmer, and the family moved to Aldridge, near Walsall, Staffordshire, about two years after Charles was born. In 1891 Charles was living with his parents, an older brother (Samuel) and a younger sister (Ursula) in High Street, Aldridge. By 1901, the family, with two younger children (Mary and Helen) lived at Manor Farm, Aldridge, with Charles being shown in the Census as a 'sailor – cadet'.

His education began in Bishop Vesey's School in Sutton Coldfield, and was continued at Coleshill Grammar School. He served for two years on the Mersey training ship, HMS *Conway* from 1899 to 1901, and then went to sea as an apprentice on the sailing vessel *Invermark*, belonging to the Aberdeen firm of George Milne & Co. He took his Master's Certificate at the early age of 22, and changed from sail to steam on joining the Johnston Line, which had a fleet of 25 ships serving the Black Sea and Mediterranean trades, as well as the USA and Canada. He was serving on the *Incemore* when she was in collision with the German liner *Kaiser Wilhelm* off the Isle of Wight.

At the outbreak of war in 1914 he was in Antwerp, Belgium, but made it back to this country and almost immediately joined the Royal Naval Division as an able seaman. He was transferred in December 1914 to the Royal Naval Reserve and appointed a Sub-Lieutenant. Recognition of his outstanding work in actions involving submarines came in July 1917 in the form of the Distinguished Service Cross. He was one of the volunteers in that very hazardous series of operations, the 'Q' ships, and it was in one of these actions while serving as First Officer to the legendary Commander Gordon Campbell VC that Charles Bonner was to earn his own medal.

The constant battle to combat the threat of the German U-boats against merchant ships brought about the use of decoy ships ('Q' ships) - armed merchant vessels whose role was to entice the U-boat to the surface within range of the decoy's concealed guns; the manner in which this was carried out was nothing short of suicidal for the crew of the merchant ship.

The converted Cardiff collier, the 'Q ship *Dunraven*, with Gordon Campbell as captain and Charles Bonner as the first officer, sailed on 4 August 1917, their destination being Queenstown in Southern Ireland. Campbell's intuition as to where U-boats possibly lurked took them towards the Bay of Biscay. On 8 August, south of Ushant, they sighted a submarine on the surface in the distance, and the first stage of their well-rehearsed performance began. They proceeded on their way as if they had not seen their prey, and the submarine watching their movement took its time in diving. When the U-boat surfaced it was astern *Dunraven*, this being the most awkward place for the collier, and the Germans opened fire at a range of about 5,000 yards. The *Dunraven* made plenty of smoke and Campbell sent off his distress signals, while his crew carried out their pantomime of being attacked on deck. The U-boat shelled for half an hour without a hit, and this caused her to close range to 1,000 yards. A near miss on the port side enabled Campbell to stop his ship, send off a lot of steam amidships, get the 'panic party' away, and turn the ship to bring the U-boat on to his beam. His chance of success suddenly disappeared when the Germans landed three shells on the *Dunraven's* poop deck. (The 'panic party' involved lowering a boat carrying an officer and crew, who would enact the part of men abandoning ship, and they would row a distance away, to lure the U-boat closer to the stricken vessel.)

The first shell that landed on the poop exploded a depth charge and blew Bonner out of his hiding place. He quickly crawled back only to find that other shells had caused a fire so that he and his men had to stay in the hide-out, as fire raged in the ammunition store below them. The U-boat became hidden in the smoke from the fire, and just as she was in Campbell's sights there was a tremendous explosion which blew Bonner and his crew and their 4-inch gun up in the air. Fortunately their lives were saved as they landed on the mock cargo on deck.

The U-boat crash dived, and Campbell attempted two shots as she went, but she was to surface again after firing a torpedo which hit the *Dunraven* just aft of the engine room. Campbell and his crew continued their act in the hope that they could draw the U-boat closer, but in spite of two more 'panic party' attempts the submarine surfaced again and proceeded to shell the *Dunraven* for some 20 minutes; then it submerged. Campbell fired two torpedoes, but they missed, and there was no response from the U-boat which had evidently expended its own stock of torpedoes and was probably short of ammunition. As help was on its way to the *Dunraven*, the submarine made its escape. The destroyer HMS *Christopher* arrived and the battered collier was taken in tow *en route* for Plymouth, but in the worsening weather the crew were taken off and she sank shortly afterwards.

The announcement of the award of the Victoria Cross to Lieutenant C.G. Bonner was given first in the Court Circular issued from York Cottage on the Sandringham estate, only the second occasion this had happened in advance of the usual *London Gazette* announcement. Bonner was instructed that the King wished to meet him and he was to go and spend the weekend at Sandringham, giving him the additional honour of being the only man who received his Victoria Cross on a Sunday from the Sovereign. The reason for this rare event was that the King had been informed that Bonner had been given command of his own 'Q' ship, and the King wanted to be sure to present him with his medal rather than to his widow at some later date. The citation was carefully phrased to give no specific details that could be of advantage to the enemy: ' For conspicuous gallantry and consummate coolness and skill in action with an enemy submarine'.

Gordon Campbell, in a similar action in March 1916, was awarded his Victoria Cross when his ship, a converted collier named *Farnborough* sank a German U-boat. A member of his crew on that occasion was Ronald Neil Stuart, who was awarded the Distinguished Service Order and the following year the Victoria Cross, again for a 'Q' boat action in the Atlantic. Stuart was born in Liverpool and features in *Liverpool Heroes* Book 1. Both Stuart and Bonner were selected by their crewmates to receive their VCs as representatives of the ships' crews. The crew of *Dunraven* selected Petty Officer Ernest Pitcher for the same award.

Bonner survived the war, and after the Armistice sailed for a short while as First Officer with the Furness Withy Line, which had taken a commercial interest in the Johnston Line. In fact, they were to buy out the Johnston Line, including Bonner's earlier ship, the *Incemore*, which was wrecked in 1940. He left and took up employment with the Leith Salvage and Towage Company and during the next 21 years became an expert in ship salvage. He was master of the tug *Bullger*, which was built the year before he was born. The Leith Salvage Co. had started in 1919, and had 24 tugs of all types on its books. One of its salvage vessels was formerly the Mersey ferry *Storeton* which, after extensive alterations, was converted into a heavy lift ship, when her shallow draught was an advantage. In the Second World War, Bonner salvaged HMS *Caledonia* (formerly the *Majestic*), at Rosyth in the Firth of Forth after she had been completely burnt out, and was called upon as a consultant in the salvage of the German battleship *Tirpitz*.

On 17 June 1917 Charles Bonner married Alice Mabel, daughter of Thomas Partridge, at the Walsall Parish Church of St. Matthew. They had a son, Gordon Dunraven Bonner, who became a Surgeon Lieutenant in the RNVR. On 9 November 1929 Bonner attended a Victoria Cross Reunion Dinner at the House of Lords and sat at the same table as John Molyneux VC who was born in St Helens.

Captain Charles George Bonner VC, DSC, RNR, died of cancer at his home in Edinburgh on 7 February 1951, aged 66 years. He was cremated at Warriston Crematorium, Edinburgh, but has a headstone in St Mary's Churchyard, Aldridge. His wife Alice died in May 1973 aged 80 years. In February 2007, Aldridge South and Streetly Local Neighbourhood Partnership called on their local council, as part of the renovation of the local war memorial, to erect a plaque to their only VC winner, Charles George Bonner. This has now been completed.

Note : Other *Conway* 'Old Boys' to be awarded the Victoria Cross included Philip Bent, Ian Fraser and Edwin Unwin, who each feature in this book.

Christopher Bushell
VC DSO

Christopher Bushell VC DSO

Born on 31 October 1888, at Hinderton Lodge, Neston, Wirral, Christopher was the younger son of Reginald Bushell and of Caroline (née Hope). His father was a partner in the family firm of Bushell Brothers & Co., wine merchants and shippers, of Castle Street, Liverpool, and was a member of the Mersey Docks and Harbour Board. Reginald Bushell, Christopher's father, was born in Aigburth. The family also lived at 2 Gambier Terrace, Liverpool before moving to Hinderton Hall and Hinderton Lodge.

Christopher Junior was educated at Moorland House, Heswall, Cheshire; at Rugby School (where he is said to have been a friend of Rupert Brooke , the war poet) and at Corpus Christi College, Oxford. He always kept in touch with his schools, and devoted much time to the Rugby Club, Notting Dale. While at Oxford he was captain of his College boat and competed at Henley.

Reginald Bushell died before the 1911 Census was taken. In that year the family, headed by Christopher's mother Caroline, was living at 59 Kensington Court in West London. This was a spacious 17-roomed house where Christopher, aged 23, was listed as a law student; his only sibling, Lilian, aged 25, was single but was not engaged in any occupation. The family of three Bushells had six domestic servants to look after them – in conclusion, the 1911 Census paints a picture of a very comfortably-off Edwardian family.

Christopher was called to the Bar in 1912.

In the same year he joined the Army, and was appointed to the Special Reserve of Officers, as a Second Lieutenant in the 1st Battalion, The Royal West Surrey Regiment. He went to France with the British Expeditionary Force, and was in the retreat from Mons, being severely wounded on 14 September 1914. He returned to France in November 1915, but in August that year had married Rachel E.F. Lambert, the elder daughter of the Vicar of Wye, Kent, the Reverend Canon E. Lambert. The ceremony was performed by the Rev. D.W. Holson MA, who was the Chaplain Superintendent of the Mersey Mission to Seamen and was also Christopher Bushell's brother-in-law. A number of RAMC men billeted in Wye at the time also attended the wedding. By now Bushell had been promoted Lieutenant.

In November 1915 he was appointed Aide de Camp to 33rd Division, remaining in this role until June 1916, when he became Staff Captain of 100th Brigade for the Battle of the Somme. In December 1916, he was appointed temporary commander of the 7th Battalion, The Queen's Royal West Surrey Regiment, becoming their Commanding Officer in January 1917, with the rank of Temporary Major, Acting Lieutenant Colonel. In September 1917, after many months in the line where they had endured some stiff fighting, his Battalion was placed in reserve and in January 1918 he was created a Companion of the Distinguished Service Order – 'For continued gallantry and devotion to duty on numerous occasions'.

Although his long confirmed rank was Captain, he was appointed Temporary Lieutenant Colonel, in command of the 7th Battalion The Queen's Royal West Surrey Regiment, and on 23 March 1918 west of the St. Quentin canal and to the north of Tergnier, he earned his Victoria Cross leading the men with whom he had been so closely associated throughout the war. His citation read:

For most conspicuous bravery and devotion to duty when in command of his battalion. Lieut. Colonel Bushell personally led 'C' Company of his battalion, who were co-operating with an Allied regiment in a counter-attack in face of very heavy machine gun fire. In the course of this attack he was severely wounded in the head, but he continued to carry on, walking about in front of both English and Allied troops, encouraging and reorganising them. He refused even to have his wound attended to until he had placed the whole line in a sound position, and formed a defensive flank to meet a turning movement by the enemy. He then went to Brigade Headquarters and reported the situation, had his wound dressed and then returned to the firing line, which had come back a short distance. He visited every portion of the line, both English and Allied, in the face of terrific machine gun and rifle fire, exhorting the troops to remain where they were and kill the enemy. In spite of his wounds this gallant officer refused, to go to the rear, and eventually had to be removed to the dressing station in a fainting condition. To the magnificent example of energy, devotion and courage shown by their commanding officer is attributed the fine spirit displayed and the keen fight put up by the men of his battalion, not only on the day in question, but on each succeeding day of the withdrawal.

On 13 May Captain (Temporary Lieutenant Colonel) Christopher Bushell was presented by the King with his Victoria Cross and his Distinguished Service Order. (Note: the Regimental website states incorrectly that his widow received his Victoria Cross from George V on 11 May 1919.) Christopher returned to the front line on 22 May 1918.

It was on the Somme, south of Morlencourt, on 8 August 1918, that this courageous man fell to a sniper's bullet to the head while leading his men against a strong enemy position. His battalion had already captured two trenches, so that he was able to share briefly in the joy of the recent great victory. He was one of the bravest and best, trusted by his superior officers and beloved by his comrades in arms and is buried in Querrieu British Cemetery, France.

On 15 June 1916, his daughter Elizabeth Hope Bushell was born, and she was baptised on 24 August, it being the first anniversary of their marriage. She became Mrs. Betsy Maclehose and lives in Scotland, as does her son.

After the death of Christopher Bushell's father, on 11 November 1904, at Hinderton Lodge, his widow and family moved to live at 'Hillside', Granville Road, St. Margaret's, at Cliffe near Dover. Later they moved to Holland Park, London. Mrs. Caroline Bushell died during the Second World War. Rachel, Christopher's widow, also moved to Wye, Kent and then to 'Hinderton', Church Road, Boughton Aluph and finally to Bishopsbourne, near Canterbury. She became a Churchwarden and was deeply involved with the Women's Voluntary

Service and was awarded an MBE in 1959. She died in 1973 and is buried in Bishopsbourne, where plaques to both Christopher and Rachel are displayed in the Parish Church.

It is likely that Christopher took his name from his grandfather, who also lived in Neston, and was a founder of the family wine trade business. Before moving to Wirral he had lived until 1853 in St. Anne's Lane, Aigburth, Liverpool, where most of his children, including Christopher's father, Reginald, were born. He is best known for his involvement in promoting elementary education in Liverpool and was the first Chairman of the Liverpool School Board under the Forster Act of 1870. He was a founder member of the Liverpool Council of Education and was President until his death in 1887. For five years he had been a Vice Chancellor of University College, forerunner of the present Liverpool University. A statue of him in marble by Albert Bruce-Joy still stands in the entrance hall of the main Victoria Building of Liverpool University. He was a great benefactor to local charities, and was also associated with the rebuilding of Neston Parish Church, as well as being Chairman of the Magistrates. The statue in Victoria Building was subscribed to by friends upon his death, with the residue of funds placed in trust to provide bursaries for new students.

(Note : in 2009 the statue of Christopher Bushell's grandfather was in storage in the Victoria Building, now the Victoria Museum and Gallery, Brownlow Hill, Liverpool. The building has been recently refurbished and the Gallery and Museum displays are still being arranged, but it is hoped that the statue will soon be uncovered and back in its rightful position. On the ground floor of the building are two memorial boards to students and staff of Liverpool University who died during the two World Wars. These include Noel Chavasse VC & Bar MC and Eric Norman Bell VC.)

Walter Norris Congreve
VC KCB MVO

Walter Norris Congreve was born on 26 November 1862 at Chatham, Kent, the eldest son of William Congreve JP DL and Fanny Emma, the daughter of Lee Porcher Townshend of Wincham Hall, Chester. William was a descendant of the Restoration playwright of the same name. The Congreve family homes were at Burton Hall, Wirral, and Congreve Manor, Staffordshire. His father had been Chief Constable of Staffordshire after an Army career and several of his ancestors had served their country in various military capacities as far back as the Civil War. Walter subsequently was to be affectionately called 'Squibs' by his contemporaries, after his grandfather, Sir William Congreve

Walter Norris Congreve VC KCB MVO

(1772-1828) who invented the 'Congreve Rocket' or 'Squib' for military use.

Walter began his education at Mr Wickham's School in Twyford, from where he went to Harrow and then to Pembroke College, Oxford. After two years he abandoned his university career and having by now served some six years in the North Staffordshire Militia he entered the Royal Military Academy at Sandhurst. In 1885 he was commissioned as a Second Lieutenant in the Rifle Brigade, joining the 1st Battalion at Belguam in India. After some months, he transferred to the 4th Battalion, missing the Burma War in which his first unit participated, and when his tour of service ended he returned to the United Kingdom. On 3 June 1890, whilst stationed at Parkhurst, Walter married Cecilia, the daughter of Captain C.B. La Touche in London. They were to have three sons, one of them being William La Touche Congreve VC. The Census of 1891 shows Walter living in Albany Barracks, Parkhurst, Hampshire, where his fellow officers included the Honourable Charles G.Fortescue, later to be GOC of the Infantry Brigade.

Promoted Captain in 1893, Walter was posted to the 3rd Battalion, Rifle Brigade, and again went off to India, returning to England in 1896, taking up a post at the Rifle Depot. In January 1898 he was appointed District Inspector of Musketry to the Aldershot Command.

On the outbreak of war in South Africa in October 1899, he resigned his appointment at Aldershot and was sent to join the 2nd Battalion, Rifle Brigade, which had been ordered from camp in Crete to Natal. Arriving in Durban, he found that his Battalion was besieged in Ladysmith and he was attached to the Staff of 4th Infantry Brigade under Sir Redvers Buller. (Coincidentally, another of his fellow officers at Albany Barracks in 1891 was the Honourable Henry Yarde Buller.)

On 15 December 1899, the 2nd Infantry Brigade crossed the Tulega River at Colenso; the 1st Field Artillery Brigade had taken up position to prepare for this attack but came under merciless fire from the Boers. The citation for Walter Congreve's Victoria Cross describes how

the detachments serving the guns of the 14th and 66th Batteries of the Royal Field Artillery had either been killed, wounded or driven from their guns by infantry fire from Boers at close range, and the guns were deserted. About 500 yards behind the guns was a donga (a narrow, steep-sided ravine) in which some of the few men and horses left alive were sheltered. The intervening space was heavily swept with shell and rifle fire and Captain Congreve, who was in the donga, assisted to hook up a team of horses into a limber, went out and assisted to limber up a gun. Being wounded, he took shelter but on seeing Lieutenant Roberts fall badly wounded, he immediately went out again to bring him in. Captain Congreve had been shot through the leg, the toe of his boot and was badly grazed on the elbow and shoulder, and his horse had been shot three times. For his conspicuous bravery, with others, in an attempt to save the guns at Colenso, he was awarded the Victoria Cross.

Lieutenant Roberts died of his wounds on 17 December 1899 and was to be the first man awarded a posthumous Victoria Cross. Another VC in the same action was awarded to George Nurse, a Liverpool resident though born in Ireland. (See Book 2 in this series.)

Walter Norris Congreve VC saw action in the Transvaal, Orange Free State and Natal and was appointed Adjutant to Kitchener's Horse and then Brigade Major to 18th Infantry Brigade. He later became Military Secretary to Lord Kitchener and in 1902 became Assistant Military Secretary (AMS) and Aide de Camp (ADC) to HRH the Duke of Connaught in Ireland. In 1903, when King Edward VII visited Ireland, Congreve was made a Member of the Royal Victorian Order (MRVO) by the King. In June 1905 he was made a Companion of the Order of the Bath (Military) and appointed Brevet Colonel. In 1906 he was posted as Second in Command of the 3rd Battalion, Rifle Brigade, at Devonport. In 1909 he was appointed Commandant of the School of Musketry at Hythe, where his South African experiences made him a fierce proponent of the need for military sharpshooters, and he was a strong supporter of the development of the machine gun. In 1911 he was given command of 18th Infantry Brigade, whose Headquarters at Lichfield were conveniently near to the then Congreve home at Chartley Castle, Staffordshire.

Walter's active military career was by no means over. At the outbreak of war in August 1914, the 18th Brigade, (part of the 6th Division), was sent to Edinburgh in case of a German attack but by 15 August had rejoined the 6th Division in Cambridge. They embarked for France in September and took part in the heavy fighting on the River Aisne. His Battalion sustained major casualties, losing some 51 officers and 1000 men. In October they moved to Flanders and became locked in desperate battles which quietened down only with the oncome of winter.

In May 1915, Walter Congreve was given command of the 6th Division, which meant he was able to remain with his old Brigade, who by now were involved in the Ypres Sector. In autumn 1915 he was promoted to the rank of Lieutenant General (Temporary) and took command of XIII Corps, now part of the Third Army. In spring 1916, he was transferred to the Fourth Army, under General Sir Henry Rawlinson, to take part in the Battle of the Somme. After initial striking success, Walter Congreve fell ill with an attack of cholera but was able to resume his command after only one month. The Corps was sent to join the First Army and in spring 1917 played a distinguished part in the Battle of Arras. In mid-June 1917, he and his Aide de Camp were inspecting the lines at the foot of Vimy Ridge when a German 5.9 High Explosive shell hit him and shattered his left hand which was subsequently amputated at a Casualty Station. Walter was sent home for further treatment and remained in England until the end of 1917. While in England, he was created a Knight Commander of the Order of the Bath (KCB) and in January 1918 was promoted to Lieutenant General in command of VII Corps, part of the Fifth Army in France under General Sir Hubert Gough.

On 21 March 1918, the Germans launched a major attack on the 5th Army's position. Despite staunch opposition in the fiercest of fighting, 5th Army was forced to withdraw after two days. The German advance succeeded only in capturing land which had been rendered a wilderness by the First Battle of the Somme and this is now widely recognised as a truly Pyrrhic victory. Allied losses totalled 255,000, mainly men who could be replaced, whilst the Germans lost 240,000 irreplaceable 'shock troops'. When VII Corps were taken out of the line to recover, Congreve was given command of X Corps near Crécy, but shortly afterwards a reorganisation of commands led to his return to England. His chronic asthma, the severe wound to his arm, the tragic loss of his son, Billy Congreve VC, in 1916 and the strain of commanding VII Corps, during which he saw his Corps sustain some 25,000 casualties, were all good reasons why Walter should be one of those chosen to leave the action zone. He had experienced his fair share of the war and had suffered greatly. He was the only Corps Commander to be wounded in the Great War and fully deserved his other nickname of 'Concrete'. By now he was 55 years old.

He remained at home on half-pay until August 1919, when he was appointed Commander of the North Force of the Egyptian Expeditionary Force under Field Marshal Edmund Henry Allenby, 1st Viscount Allenby, widely known as the 'Bloody Bull', with a reputation for tyrannical control of his troops. Shortly afterwards, Walter was appointed General Officer Commanding (GOC) Egyptian Expeditionary Force, with his headquarters in Cairo, where he remained until 1923. In 1922 he had been promoted to General and was Colonel in Chief, 1st Battalion Rifle Brigade.

On his return to England, he became GOC Southern Command with his headquarters at Salisbury and on 29 June 1925 succeeded Field Marshal Lord Plumer as Governor of Malta and its Dependencies. (Plumer was to lay the foundation stone of St George's Memorial Church in Ypres and to inaugurate the Menin Gate Memorial in 1927). In 1926, with his wife, Walter Congreve went to Italy in the hope that this would be beneficial for his asthma but sadly he developed bronchitis and pneumonia. In 1927, in hospital at Imtarfa, Malta, he suffered heart problems and dropsy and died there on 27 February. He was buried at sea between the Malta mainland and the island of Filfila on 4 March 1927.

Walter Congreve was a tall, gaunt man whose recreations had included polo, fishing and small game hunting. He also had a keen interest in Church architecture. He was a keen but fair disciplinarian and in the Front Line was regularly to be found amongst his troops in the trenches, ensuring for himself that all was as well as it could be. When his son, William la Touche Congreve, won his Victoria Cross, they became only the third case of father and son to have done so. The others are Major C.J.S.Gough (Indian Mutiny 1857-8) and Brevet Major J. E. Gough (Somaliland 1903), and Lieutenant F.S. Roberts (Indian Mutiny) and Lieutenant the Honourable F.H.S. Roberts (South Africa 1899). When Walter Norris, Freddy Roberts and George Nurse won their VCs at Colenso, a fourth was awarded to William, later Sir William Babtie, Royal Army Medical Corps. Another officer, Captain (later Lieutenant Colonel) Harry Norton Schofield, from Ashton under Lyne, was awarded the Distinguished Service Order (DSO). Schofield was Aide de Camp to General Sir Redvers Buller who said in his report: 'I have differentiated in my recommendations because I thought that the Victoria Cross required proof of initiative, something more in fact than mere obedience to orders', inferring that Schofield had merely been obeying orders. A Press campaign and public outcry eventually resulted in the cancellation of Schofield's DSO and the award of the Victoria Cross in August 1901. Schofield's medals were sold in auction at Sotheby's, together with his sword, in November 1888 for £15,000, and his VC is now part of Lord Ashcroft's collection. Walter Congreve's VC is held by the Royal Green Jackets Museum in Winchester.

Walter's wife Cecilia served with the nursing service in Antwerp in 1914 and was one of the last to leave, on a London omnibus full of wounded troops. She received a *Reconnaissance Française* from the French Government and later, in recognition of her courage and coolness when her hospital at Rosières-aux-

Salines near Nancy was bombed, was awarded the French *Croix de Guerre*. For her services in Belgium, the King of the Belgians awarded her the Queen Elizabeth Medal. Born in 1867, she died in 1952. Her father, Lieutenant C.B.la Touche, on 3 November 1857 during the Indian Mutiny assisted in the rescue under extreme circumstances of a wounded comrade and was recommended for the Victoria Cross. While his gallantry was noted, the award was not authorised. If it had been, Cecilia would have had the unique distinction of being the daughter of one Victoria Cross holder, the wife of another and the mother of a third!

William La Touche Congreve VC DSO MC

William Congreve was born on 22 March 1891, at his grandfather's home, Burton Hall, Wirral, the eldest son of Walter Norris Congreve VC and Cecilia Henrietta Dolores Congreve (née La Touche). He was educated in Farnborough at a school run by Miss Sara Linton and between 1902 and 1904 at Summerfield School, Oxford, a boys' prep school run by Archibald Maclaren (a fencing expert), his wife, Gertrude, their daughters and sons in law. A fellow pupil at the time was Harold Macmillan, later to become Prime Minister. Another former pupil was the actor, Christopher Lee. Congreve then went to Eton before spending some time at a 'crammer' school before entering Sandhurst in

William La Touche Congreve VC DSO MC

1909. On leaving, he was runner-up to the cadet awarded Sandhurst's Sword of Honour.

In 1911 he joined the 3rd Battalion of the Rifle Brigade in Tipperary as a Second Lieutenant and spent what he described as three happy years, leading up to the 1914 War. Promoted to Lieutenant on 1 February 1913, he went to France with the 6th Division, landing at St. Nazaire on 12 September 1914. They made their way up to the Front by transport and then marched 60 miles to join in the Battle of the Aisne. On 21 September he was selected to be Aide De Camp (A.D.C.) to General Hubert Hamilton of the 3rd Division and a successful drive northwards after the Aisne battle took him to Abbeville *en route* for Flanders.

The fighting at this time was hard and desperate, and on 14 October near Armentières a sniper's bullet killed General Hamilton while he was in the line with his troops. Hamilton was the first British Divisional Commander to die in the Great War. His replacement was Major General MacKenzie, who had no success in the ensuing battle for Neuve Chapelle, resulting in his recall to England. Command was now given to Major General F.D.V. Wing, so in less than six weeks Billy Congreve had been ADC to three commanders. (Wing was himself killed in action near Loos on 2 October 1915.)

The First Battle of Ypres began on 11 November 1914, and the 3rd Division, whose troops had been in the thick of the fighting almost since their arrival in France, was now stationed in the Salient area. Comprised of 7,850 battle-weary troops, they were defending their position against the élite Prussian Guards and the German 4th Division, who numbered 17,500 men, supported by 228 guns. The battle was fiercely fought and continued up to 21 November with the enemy gaining little ground, when the line was taken over by the French. Billy Congreve had worked tirelessly in his role in the front line since September and was now ordered to take a short leave because of a throat infection.

Winter rain, snow and bitter winds curtailed the activities of both sides but the 3rd Division was eventually moved into the line embracing St. Eloi, just south of Ypres. It was now March 1915, and preparations were well in hand for the Second Battle of Ypres. Young Billy Congreve was soon to experience one of the most horrifying weapons ever used: poison gas. It was deployed on the north eastern front of the Salient in April 1915, and hit the French and Canadians with devastating effect; the sight of so many young men suffering intolerable and lasting agony etched this battle into the minds of men for evermore. In *Tommy* (2005) Richard Holmes quotes Company Sergeant Major Ernest Shephard of the 1st Dorsetshire Regiment, who describes the effects of a gas attack on Hill 60:

> *The scene that followed was heartbreaking. Men were caught by fumes and in dreadful agony, coughing and vomiting, rolling on the ground in agony... I ran round at intervals and tied up lots of men's mouths, placed them in sitting positions, and organized parties to assist them to the support dugouts... When we found our men were dying from fumes we wanted to charge, but were not allowed to do so.*

What a start for May. Hell could find no worse than the groans of scores of dying and badly hurt men... Hardly know who is dead yet, but several of my best chums are gone under...The Dorset Regiment's motto is now 'No prisoners'. No quarter will be given when we again get to fighting.

Billy Congreve was a key figure in the area for much of the campaign, being responsible for several successful operations and was Mentioned in Dispatches by Sir John French on two occasions. On 15 October 1915, he was awarded the *Croix de Chevalier, Légion d'Honneur* by the French Government and received this accolade in front of a parade of British and French troops, from General de Boiselle. Among the onlookers was his father - a moment of proud satisfaction for both men.

About three miles outside of Ypres was the mining village of Hooge, which had been in the possession of both sides at least twice. Hooge was the scene of a number of very fierce battles, in one of which the Germans used flame-throwers which literally burned men alive. Captain Noel Chavasse earned his Military Cross here in June 1915 and it was in an attack on Hooge in November 1915, that Billy Congreve won his Military Cross.

On 8 December 1915, Billy Congreve was made Brigade Major of the 76th Infantry Brigade, and this was followed by his third Mention in Despatches, this time from Sir Douglas Haig. On 27 March 1916, British troops mounted an attack with the object of trying to straighten out the line at St. Eloi and cut away the small German salient which encroached on the semi-circle of the British line in the area of the craters south of the town. The attack had commenced at 2 am in fog so thick that many Allied troops lost their way across the muddy ground and the attack almost failed, but they had pushed the enemy back. In the confused situation, the British had bypassed one crater in which a number of Germans had been cut off and were now to the British rear so that they were able to cause problems for the troops. Congreve took the initiative and determined to find out how many enemy were in the crater. With another officer and four men in support, he went forward over the 50 or so yards of open ground towards the edge of the crater, a shot being fired at him as he went. On reaching the crater he was amazed to find that it was almost full of armed Germans. He leveled his revolver and ordered them to surrender, and more than 70 officers and men climbed out and were escorted away. He was recommended for the Victoria Cross for conspicuous bravery in consolidating a newly-won position and capturing 72 Germans. However, he was instead awarded the Distinguished Service Order for this action.

A great deal of reorganisation on the front line was to take place in the coming months of 1916, as preparations for the Somme offensive were put in hand, and Billy Congreve, now a Brevet Major with the 3rd Division, found himself in XIII Corps under the command of his father as part of the Fourth Army under General Rawlinson. They moved into the line facing Montauban. The British artillery commenced bombardment of the German lines on 24 June, and during the following seven days some 70 minor infantry raids were made to ascertain the enemy's disposition. This great build up and the work of preparation brought a new eagerness to Billy Congreve but this was quickly deflated when he found that his Brigade was to be held in reserve on the opening day of what is known as the Battle of the Somme, 1 July 1916, arguably the single most bloody day of battle ever fought by the British Army.

By nightfall on the first day British forces had suffered casualties of over 60,000 men, and the gain in terms of territory recovered was negligible. Ironically, only the 30th Division of Billy's father, General W.N. Congreve, part of XIII Corps and commanded by his brother-in-law, Major General John Shea, achieved its objective of capturing and clearing Montauban. It was a vital gain that W.N. Congreve wanted dearly to exploit, but General Rawlinson restrained them and ordered them to consolidate. Because of the terrible battering given to the 18th Division, it was relieved by the 3rd Division and young Congreve moved up into the front line on 6 July. Over the next fourteen days he was to demonstrate a most remarkable display of military skill and outright courage that was to earn him the highest award, but sadly, at the cost of his life.

The *London Gazette* of 26 October 1916 announced his award thus:

> *Brevet Major William La Touche Congreve DSO, MC, The Rifle Brigade, for most conspicuous gallantry during a period of fourteen days preceding his death in action.*

> *This officer constantly performed acts of gallantry and showed the greatest devotion to duty, and by his personal example inspired all those around him with confidence at critical periods of the operations. During preliminary preparations for the attack he carried out personal reconnaissances of the enemy lines, taking out*

parties of officers and non-commissioned officers for over 1,000 yards in front of our line, in order to acquaint them with the ground. All these preparations were made under fire.

Later by night, Major Congreve conducted a battalion to its position of employment, afterwards returning to it to ascertain the situation after assault. He established himself in an exposed forward position from which he successfully observed the enemy, and gave orders necessary to drive them from their position. Two days later, when Brigade Headquarters was heavily shelled and many casualties resulted, he went out and assisted the Medical Officer to remove the wounded to places of safety, although he himself was suffering severely from gas and other shell effects. Again, on a subsequent occasion he showed supreme courage in tending wounded under shell fire. He finally returned to the front line to ascertain the situation after an unsuccessful attack, and whilst in the act of writing his report was shot and killed instantly.

Thus, at Longueval on the Somme on 20 July 1916, was ended the life of a young man with the energy, ability and determination to have become a truly great soldier. No other officer had previously ever won the VC, DSO, and MC. He was buried in the military cemetery at Corbie, and his father General W.N. Congreve VC, commanding XIII Corps, attended his funeral.

Billy had married Pamela Cynthia Maude, daughter of Cyril Maude and his wife 'Miss Winifred Emery', who were well known theatrical entertainers. They were married on 1 June 1916, at St. Martins-in-the-Fields , London, the Bishop of London, and the Reverend H.R.L. (Dick) Sheppard officiating. They had one daughter, Mary Gloria, who was born in 1917 and christened at St. Paul's Cathedral, London in April that year. Following her husband's death after only two months of married life, Pamela remarried in December 1919, her new husband being Brigadier the Honourable William Fraser, son of Lord Salton of Abernethy. Billy's medals were sent to Mrs. W.Fraser, Inverar, Nairn, Scotland. In 1930, Pamela Fraser and Lieutenant Colonel L.H.Thornton published their book *The Congreves – Father and Son*.

Billy Congreve's headstone in Corbie Communal Cemetery Extension near Arras, is inscribed as follows:

MAJOR W. LA TOUCHE CONGREVE

VC DSO MC

RIFLE BRIGADE

20 JULY 1916

LEGION D'HONNEUR

IN REMEMBRANCE OF MY BELOVED HUSBAND AND IN GLORIOUS EXPECTATION

There is also a memorial tablet, inscribed in French and designed by Sir Edwin Lutyens RA, in Corbie Church. The Congreve family motto is very appropriate: *Non moritur cujus fama vivet* - 'He dies not, whose fame survives'.

For many years, Billy's decorations and a miniature portrait of him were displayed at the Royal Green Jackets Museum, Winchester. In 1983, his daughter, living in Marbella, Spain, wrote to the custodians of the Regimental Museum and requested them to sell her father's awards. The museum launched a memorial fund to save the precious items of regimental history and at auction by Sotheby's on 30 June 1983 his medals were sold for the sum of £26,000. On 30 April 2004, Spinks Auctioneers sold the collection of John Devonport, including Walter Norris Congreve's sword and scabbards, presented to him after he earned his VC at Colenso in December 1899 and which he had given to his son, Billy, when the latter joined his father's Regiment in 1911. This sword is probably the only one ever to have belonged to two winners of the Victoria Cross and was sold with a photograph of Billy wearing it, together with other photographs and letters. Billy's Victoria Cross is now on display in the Museum of the Royal Green Jackets at Winchester.

Billy Congreve's military record was outstanding. Despite such a short life, he earned praise from all ranks, from private to field marshal, and his genuine modesty and concern for others, together with his great natural courage, epitomise the best of British manhood.

The 'Front Line Scout'

Billy Congreve's younger brother, Geoffrey, born in 1897, enlisted in the Royal Navy, attained the rank of Lieutenant Commander and served on the battleship HMS *Benbow*.

His youngest brother Arthur Christopher John was involved in what must have been one of the most bizarre situations ever to have happened. *Armageddon Road – A VC's Diary 1914-1916 by Billy Congreve*, edited by Terry Norman (1982), describes what took place:

> *(At the front) having recently said farewell to his son Geoffrey, Billy Congreve's father was surprised to be visited by his youngest son, Christopher John, then aged twelve and dressed in his Boy Scout uniform. Christopher was spending his school summer holidays in France helping his mother who was nursing at the Anglo-American Hospital at Ris-Orangis, just south of Paris. According to Christopher Congreve, who in later life joined the Rifle Brigade (retiring in 1946 with the rank of Major), his greatest adventure on that holiday was visiting the front line and walking along it with his father, coming in for the odd crump and burst of small arms fire - this must have intrigued the soldiery for, coming round a traverse and finding the two of them, one was heard to exclaim: 'Blimey, Bill – here's a bleedin' Boy Scaht!'*

It is possible that Christopher was the youngest British person to visit any Great War front during the action. We have all heard of children wanting to see father at his work, but this was taking it a little too far!

Note: William Congreve is one of 39 Old Etonians to have been awarded the Victoria Cross – 13 of them, including Congreve, during the Great War. The most recent Old Etonian VC winner was Colonel 'H' Jones during the Falklands War in 1982.

Edgar Christopher Cookson VC DSO

E dgar Cookson was born on 13 December 1883, at Cavendish Park, Tranmere, Wirral, the son of Captain William Edgar de Crackenthorpe Cookson RN and Louise Helene, a naturalized German born in Wurttemberg. His father was the Admiralty pilot on the Mersey, an onerous and responsible position then as now, because of the river currents and channels. By 1891, the family had moved to Clifton Wood, Bristol. Edgar was educated at Hazelhurst School, Frant, near Tonbridge Wells, in Kent, and in September 1897 joined HMS *Britannia* as a Naval Cadet. *Britannia*, a Royal Navy Training Ship, was previously called HMS *Prince of Wales* and was eventually broken up in 1916. In 1899 Cookson served

Edgar Christopher Cookson VC DSO

under Captain Philip F. Tillard as a midshipman on HMS *Dido* on the China Station and later in the Boxer Rebellion of 1902. He was promoted to Lieutenant in 1906 and on 30 September 1913 was appointed Lieutenant Commander, second-in-command on the sloop HMS *Clio* on the China Station.

When war broke out in 1914, Cookson was immediately involved, and spent the latter part of 1914 and the early part of 1915 serving in the European theatre; he then took part in the defence of the Suez Canal before being attached to the Mesopotamian Expeditionary Force operating in the Persian Gulf. The Turks had entered the war on the side of Germany, and British interests, including the

Persian oilfields, were deemed to be at risk, so an Expeditionary Force was mobilised from India to be landed in the area of Shatt-el-Arab, where the two great rivers Tigris and Euphrates converge to flow together into the sea. By July 1915, in a rapid movement, the area and the oil town of Basra were in the hands of the British. This would have been enough to satisfy our interests in the area but the temptation to drive further northwards and capture Baghdad committed the Expeditionary Force to a course of action that was to be tragic in the extreme.

Naval support in all of these operations was carried out by one of the most unlikely looking naval flotillas ever assembled anywhere. There was a need for vessels of shallow draught that could be navigated up the Tigris and give armed support to the artillery, and could also enable supplies to keep up with the advance, and a collection of river gunboats from the China Station, paddle steamers, stern wheelers, launches, tugs, and a variety of lighters and barges was amassed. It was within this motley group that Cookson found himself.

On 9 May 1915, Lieutenant Commander Cookson was conducting a reconnaissance up a creek of the River Euphrates, west of Qurnah, in the armed launch *Shushan*, when he was heavily attacked by Arabs concealed in the reeds. The guns, rifles and machine guns on board the cumbersome old steam launch swept the enemy positions on the river banks as the vessel was turned about to get out of this hostile spot. Cookson had been severely wounded early in the fight, but as soon as his wound was roughly dressed he took charge of the launch to ensure the safety of the vessel and his crew as he coolly navigated her back down the difficult river. He not only extricated his ship and crew from a perilous position but was able to report valuable information on the strength and disposition of the enemy. For his role in this operation he was created a Companion of the Distinguished Service Order, on 13 September 1915.

The advance towards Baghdad continued but not at the rate achieved in the initial landings as the Turks and Arabs combined to offer the toughest resistance in the most uncompromising conditions. The motley flotilla had given sterling service in its support of the land forces and had played a major part in the capture of El Amara, on the River Tigris, in June. The next objective on this river was the town of Kut, some 120 miles up-river, and the battle for this town and fort commenced on 26 September. The land forces comprising British and Indian troops under General Townsend had driven the enemy in front of them, but the Turks had thrown a formidable defensive boom across the Tigris which would cause serious problems with supplies. Townsend requested that the naval force should try to clear the obstacle. The enemy had run two iron barges aground on either bank of the river linking them by heavy cables to a native dhow which had been sunk in midstream. This obstacle and the surrounding banks were targeted by the Turkish artillery and by well-positioned machine gun and rifle fire. On 28 September 1915 the Acorn Class destroyer HMS *Comet*, commanded by Lieutenant Commander Cookson DSO, RN, with two armed launches, *Sumana* and *Shaitan*, was ordered to examine the obstruction and if possible destroy it.

As the gunboats were approaching the barrier, very heavy machine gun and rifle fire were encountered from the enemy on the banks. An attempt to sink the dhow in the centre of the river by gunfire from the vessels failed and Edgar Cookson ordered the *Comet* to be placed alongside it. As the gunboat charged the dhow, he personally jumped down with an axe to try to sever the cables. He was completely exposed to the enemy fire and was hit almost immediately. As he struggled to deliver his blow he was hit several more times. He was dragged back on board and died shortly afterwards, but not before he told his men to turn back and save themselves and their ships. The *Comet* had received serious damage to her guns and there were many casualties amongst her crew, but the three vessels were able to escape further damage as they sailed out of range. (*Comet* was eventually torpedoed and sunk by a German U-boat in the Mediterranean on 6 August 1918.)

The British ground artillery reached the area and the Turks moved away during the night so that next morning all was quiet, and the tragic irony of Edgar Cookson's courageous efforts was that the obstacles were removed in complete safety within 24 hours of his death. He was awarded the Victoria Cross, posthumously, for an act of conspicuous gallantry. This was gazetted on 21 January 1916.

Cookson was unmarried, and his father had died years earlier, so his mother, as next of kin received his Cross from the King on 29 November 1916. At this time she was living at 15, Park Royal, Clifton, Bristol but the Census of 1901 shows her living with her daughter Eveline and son-in-law Charles Spence at 1 Albert Road, Bristol, which was then the address of Clifton College. Charles was a schoolmaster born in Rock Ferry.

(Clifton College, founded in 1862, has had a number of illustrious Old Boys, including Field Marshal Sir Douglas Haig. Sir Michael Redgrave and John Cleese are amongst former pupils, although the latter is said to have been expelled.) Another coincidence is that Sir Henry Newbold attended the college before going on to write his famous poem 'Vitas Lampada', in which he compares a cricket match with a battle in the Great War with the well-known lines : ' 'The voice of a schoolboy rallies the ranks, Play up! Play up! And Play the game!' The cricket field at the College is called 'The Close' and the opening lines of the same poem read :

There's a deadly hush in the Close tonight,

Ten to make and the match to win!

W.G.Grace is said to have scored 13 centuries on the Close whilst representing Gloucestershire. During the Second World War the college was evacuated and the buildings used by US commanders to plan the landing at Omaha Beach. Since then the School has flown the American flag.)

Edgar Cookson was buried in Amara War Cemetery, Iraq. In 1933, the headstones in the cemetery were found to have deteriorated in the salty soil and had to be removed, so the graves remain unmarked. Cookson's name does however appear on a panel of the memorial within the cemetery. His medals are privately held.

Edgar's father had at one time served on the paddle sloop HMS *Sphinx*, also on the China Station, and it was on this vessel that George Hinckley VC earned his medal in 1862. (See Book 1 in this series.)

$\mathcal{J}$ack Thomas Counter VC

Jack Thomas Counter VC

Jack Thomas Counter was born on 3 November 1898, at Blandford Forum, Dorset, the son of cabinet maker Frank and his wife Rosina Counter. The 1901 Census shows Frank and Rosina, with their three children (Percy born c.1895, Gertrude born c.1897 and Thomas J. born c.1899) living at 15 Queens Road, Pimperne, Dorset.

Jack, the 'Thomas J' mentioned above, was educated at Blandford National School and became apprenticed to the International Stores (now part of Gateway) but did not complete his apprenticeship, joining the army in February 1917, as a private. He was eventually posted to the 1st Battalion King's Liverpool Regiment (KLR) and after initial training was sent to join the regiment in France. It was not long before he received his baptism of fire in the bloody horrors of war.

The 1st Battalion KLR had spent much of 1917 in the Ypres Salient, and had taken part in some really rough battles, but it was not until 1918 that young Jack Counter was to make his mark. In March of that year General Erich von Ludendorff, who with Hindenburg was directing the German Army, suggested and launched a massive offensive on the Aisne and Marne and around Bapaume and for a while it was touch and go whether the Allied lines could withstand the assault. They managed to hold out and reserves were rushed into the various points of weakness arising from the numbers of casualties. The KLR was not involved in the Marne battle of 1918 (in fact no King's Battalion was to engage in a major operation in the 1918 campaign until August) but they were involved in many of the raids and counter-raids in the area. Both sides conducted these harassment raids to hinder the opposition's attempts to stabilize their lines and the King's were in action at Poperinghe, Givenchy, Festubert, Arras and elsewhere. In April 1918, the 1st Bn KLR was holding a precarious section of the front line in the vicinity of Moyenneville, a village south of Arras and about half way between it and Bapaume. Lt.Colonel Burke-Gaffney in his book *The Story of the King's Regiment* explains that there was no communication trench leading from their position to the front line and the only way to reach it from the rear was across some 250 yards of open country. A sunken road led through the position and out into No Man's Land from Boyelles across to Boisleux St. Marc. Down this road early on 16 April 1918 the enemy made a concerted raid on the King's. This began with a heavy artillery barrage of 4-inch and 6-inch shells together with intense trench mortar fire and then the German infantry in great numbers moved rapidly into an unoccupied trench and began bombing operations. There were heavy casualties in the King's lines, and it looked almost as if they were to be overrun. Our own artillery then began shelling the road to stem the enemy numbers causing a great many casualties among the enemy but by 10 am the Germans occupied some 400 yards of the front trench. An attack by 'B' Company at one end and by the Canadians at the other, with some bitter fighting, led to about 200 yards of trench being recovered. An hour later the Germans attempted another attack down the sunken road but were again beaten back by machine gun fire. After a lull, they tried again but once more the pattern was repeated. Enemy bombardment meant that there was no communication with Battalion Headquarters and the nature of the ground to be covered meant that no messages had got through. The only way to Headquarters was along the trenches and down a sunken road and then down a forward slope for about 250 yards, with no cover and in full view of the enemy, who was sweeping the whole area with machine gun fire.

A small party tried to make the run but was cut down, the leader and another man being killed outright. Single runners then attempted to get through but on each occasion they were killed in full sight of their comrades. Aware that five men had been thus killed, Private Jack Counter volunteered to attempt to take the message. He went out knowing full well what had gone before and under terrific enemy fire. Fate was kind to him for he got through unscathed. He then returned with the vital information that enabled his Commanding Officer to organize and launch a counter-attack, which regained the lost ground. Later, undaunted by the obvious danger, Counter repeated his terrifying ordeal on no less than five occasions, despite the heavy artillery barrage splattering the ground around him. His courage, knowing he was risking certain death, was extraordinary but he knew how vital it was that the messages were delivered. Many of Jack Counter's colleagues were young soldiers, brought in to replace the casualties sustained in March that year and there is no doubt that his courage was an inspiration to such young and untried men.

This young man, a mere nineteen years of age, had shown courage and devotion to duty beyond his years and deservedly earned his Victoria Cross. On 28 June 1918, after his investiture by King George V at Buckingham Palace, he went home on leave to Blandford to be met by the Mayor and Corporation and was given a tumultuous welcome. He had the additional honour of being the first Honorary Freeman of the Borough of Blandford Forum. When asked about his exploits, he frequently reminded questioners that, in his view, the Cross should have been awarded to the five brave men who had died attempting that which he had done. This modesty and friendliness made him well-liked wherever he was.

His regiment went to Jersey in 1919 and when he was demobilised in 1922, he joined the Post Office as an auxiliary postman at St. Ouen. He transferred in 1925 to Sunbury Common, Middlesex, to become established in the postal service before returning to Jersey to take up a town round. It is known that he attended a VC Garden Party on 26 June 1920 and a dinner at the House of Lords in 1929, when he shared a table with two other local VC winners, namely Edward Unwin (page 91 in this volume) and Ronald Neil Stuart (Book 1 in this series). His Victoria Cross is displayed in the Jersey Museum, St Helier.

Jack Counter married and had a daughter; their family home was 'Conamar', Hansford Land, First Tower, St Helier. They lived there through the German occupation during the Second World War, and he retired from the Post Office on 11 April 1959. He did some work afterwards for G.D. Laurens, of Queen Street and Bath Street, who owned fishing vessels, and then with R. LeBail & Co., wine and beer importers, of Grenville Street. He played an active role in the affairs of the British Legion, and was standard bearer on many occasions at the Festival of Remembrance attended by both King George VI and by the present Queen. Both his daughter and his wife predeceased him, his wife by only a few months. On a visit to relatives in Blandford, Counter was taken ill and died shortly afterwards, on 16 September 1970. After cremation in

Bournemouth, his ashes were returned to St. Helier, Jersey. There is a plaque near the war memorial of St. Andrews and a headstone in the churchyard of St Saviour's, Helier, where a housing development is named 'Jack Counter Close' in his memory. In 1971, it being the 50th Anniversary of the foundation of the British Legion, a special commemorative 7 pence postage stamp was issued by the Jersey Post Office which depicted Jack Counter and his Victoria Cross.

On 20 August 1972, members of the Jersey Branch of the Old Contemptibles held their annual commemorative service at St. Andrew's Church, First Tower and were joined by members of the Jersey Branch of the British Legion. During the service, a plaque in memory of Jack Counter VC was dedicated. The plaque was the gift of the British Legion for whom he had been standard-bearer. The wife of the Lieutenant Governor, Lady Davis, attended. Her husband unfortunately was indisposed but his ADC and his secretary were present together with many local notables. The Dean of Jersey, the Very Reverend T.A. Goss, who had been a prisoner of the Japanese in the Second World War, summed up the qualities of Jack Counter with the lines from a poem 'The Prayer of a Soldier':

I'm but the son my mother bore,

But - God of strength and gentleness,

Be pleased to make me nothing less.

(**Footnote**: Blandford Forum, Dorset, was largely destroyed by fire in 1731 but over the next 30 years or so was rebuilt under the supervision of John and William Bastard and is now recognized as a near perfect example of Georgian building of that period. This explains the inscription on paving stones outside Blandford Town Hall of the following lines:

Recipe for Regeneration –

Take one careless

Tallow Chandler and

Two ingenious Bastards!).

*J*ohn Thomas Davies
VC

Born on 29 September 1895, at 19 Railway Road, Tranmere, Birkenhead, John Thomas Davies was the eldest son of general labourer John Davies, and of Margaret (née Hughes) from Mostyn, Flintshire, who married in Birkenhead in 1884. While John was still an infant the family moved to St. Helens, Lancashire, where his father obtained employment as a platelayer at Cannington Shaw's glass bottle works. In 1901, John and Margaret were living with their four children (Margaret, 11; Esther, 7; John T., 6; and Thomas, 4) at 5 Sutton Heath Road, St Helens. In the 1911 Census the family occupied a three-roomed house at 22 Essex Street. John Thomas Davies was educated at Arthur Street

John Thomas Davies VC

School in St. Helens, and on leaving there worked as a labourer at a local colliery (1911 Census). He subsequently took employment with the Ravenhead Sanitary Brick and Pipe Works.

He was one of the first St. Helens youths to join the South Lancashire Regiment's 'Pals' Battalions when they were formed in September 1914. He was posted to the 11th Battalion and remained in this country on defence and training on Salisbury Plain until November 1915 when they were sent to France. Through the winter of that year there was little action and the rain and snow made life pretty miserable for those in the trenches, but in the spring of 1916 he was to be involved in almost constant fighting. He was wounded twice in the many battles on the Somme front but recovered to continue back in the front line. Apart from some leave he remained in the thick of the fray, and during the great German Spring push in 1918 Corporal John Thomas Davies earned the coveted Victoria Cross.

On 20 March 1918, the Germans launched their attack (Operation Michael) at four objectives along the front line: Arras in the northern area; Croiselles and Bullecourt; Bapaume and Peronne; and in the south from St. Quentin. It was to be the move to finish the war with one final thrust towards the Channel ports. The weather on that opening day with rain on the warming ground sent a dense mist across most of the front line. Supported by a massive artillery barrage, the Germans drenched the British forward positions with poison gas, and were able to break through in a number of vital places. In the area of St. Quentin they were able to break the link between the British and French lines and it was here that the fighting became one of survival for the British units who were forced against overwhelming numbers to begin withdrawing. The Allies had been taken by surprise and were completely outnumbered in terms of men and equipment, but they fought magnificently, and time and again attempted counter-attacks to delay the German advance. In one week of fighting, the Battalion lost almost 420 men, approximately 50% of its effective strength. That any were able to escape was due to the bravery and tenacity of their Lewis Gunners, who stayed at their guns until either killed or wounded. Such were the conditions in which the 11th Battalion of the South Lancashire Regiment fought its rearguard action at Eppeville, some 13 miles to the south-west of St. Quentin. The award of the Victoria Cross to John Davies was gazetted on 23 May 1918 :

Corporal John Thomas Davies, for most conspicuous bravery and devotion to duty under heavy rifle and machine-gun fire (on 24 March 1918). When his company - outflanked on both sides - received orders to withdraw, Corporal Davies knew that the only line of withdrawal lay through a deep stream lined with a belt of barbed wire and that it was imperative to hold up the enemy as long as possible. He mounted the parapet, fully exposing himself to enemy guns, in order to get a more effective field of fire, and kept his Lewis gun in action to the last, causing the enemy many casualties and checking their advance. By his very great devotion to duty he enabled part of his company to get across the river, which they would otherwise have been unable to do, thus undoubtedly saving the lives of many of his comrades. When last seen this gallant NCO was still firing his gun, with the enemy close on top of him, and was in all probability killed at his gun.

His award was a posthumous one, but it transpired that in spite of the desperate situation that he was in when last seen by his comrades - the enemy having all but completely surrounded him, and that he was still firing as they made their escape across the Somme - he had in fact been captured and sent to a prison camp at Zagan, in Silesia (now Poland). It was a great shock to his parents to be informed of his posthumous award, and even more of a shock to receive a postcard from him later in the year to say that he was a prisoner of war! He received a very special welcome on his return to his home in Alma Street, Peasley Cross, St. Helens.

The circumstances of the award being made and his receipt of the Victoria Cross are unique. I understand that no amendment was ever made to his citation which makes him the only person to have lived to accept a posthumous V.C.

John Thomas Davies' grave at St Helens Borough Cemetery

A quiet, reserved man, John rarely spoke of his experiences in the war. He married Beatrice and they had a son and daughter. It is believed that he returned to his former employers after his discharge when the battalion was disbanded. In peacetime he was acquainted with another holder of the Victoria Cross who came from the same neighbourhood in St. Helens - John Molyneux. They attended various functions together, and in the 1930s were amongst a number of ex-servicemen who were presented to the then Prince of Wales (later Edward VIII). On Saturday 19 July 1924, King George V and Queen Mary visited Liverpool for the consecration of the Anglican Cathedral. Also present was Bishop Chavasse, father of Noel Godfrey Chavasse VC & Bar MC. That afternoon the King reviewed the 55th West Lancashire Territorial Division at Wavertree Playground, Liverpool. Amongst nine VC holders who attended were John Davies and John Molyneux. Both men had also attended a Victoria Cross Reunion Garden Party in June 1920, their signatures appearing on a menu for that occasion which was later sold at auction. During the Second World War Davies and Molyneux both served in the Home Guard – Davies with the 75th Bn of the West Lancashire Home Guard, and Molyneux in the Pilkington Glass Battalion.

Davies died suddenly on 28 October 1955, at the early age of sixty years. His wife Beatrice died in 1976 aged 85 years and is buried with her husband and their son, Alan, who died in 1943 aged only 20 years, in St Helens Borough Cemetery. His Victoria Cross is displayed in the Imperial War Museum.

Footnotes:

The place where Davies earned his VC, Eppeville, was less than twenty miles from the town of St. Gobain, noted for its glass industry and with close associations with Pilkington Bros. Limited of St. Helens.

A photograph held by Warrington Museum but originating from the South Lancashire Regimental Museum features Davies with three other South Lancashire Regiment VC winners – William Ratcliffe and Gabriel Coury (see Book 1 in this series) and John Readitt. Unfortunately to date it has not been possible to ascertain when, where or why the photograph was taken – nevertheless it is a wonderful group of men! Perhaps it was taken before they were presented to their Majesties on 19 July 1924? The photograph is reprinted on page 99 of this book.

Charles Calveley Foss
VC DSO

harles Foss was born on 9 March 1885 at Kobe, then the chief port of Japan, close to the industrial city of Osaka, where his father, the Right Reverend Hugh James Foss was Bishop. Charles Foss's grandfather, Edward Foss, born in 1789, was a Justice of the Peace for Kent and Surrey and the author of works on legal history and various biographies. His mother, Janet, who died in 1894, was the daughter of Doctor William McEwen of Chester. By 1871, the family had moved to live in Croydon, when Hugh James was an undergraduate of Cambridge University and his mother was by now widowed.

Charles Calveley Foss VC DSO

From 1899 to 1902 Charles Foss was educated at Marlborough College, founded in 1843 for the education of sons of Church of England clergy, from where he gained entry to the Royal Military Academy, Sandhurst. He was commissioned on 2 March 1904, joining the Bedfordshire Regiment. After various tours of duty he was promoted to Captain, in the 2nd Battalion, in 1912 and at the outbreak of war in 1914 was with his Regiment in South Africa. Marlborough School has a proud military tradition, counting no fewer than 14 recipients of the Victoria Cross amongst its Old Boys. Other Old Boys include John Betjeman (poet), Antony Blunt (spy), Siegfried Sassoon (poet), James Mason and James Robertson Justice (actors) and Sir Francis Chichester (yachtsman).

On 1 January 1915 Foss was awarded the Distinguished Service Order for his deeds during the First Battle of Ypres, when he was the only one of four officers to survive. Two months later, on 12 March 1915, he took part in the Battle of Neuve Chapelle, a village south-west of Lille. This battle lasted for three days from 10 to 12 March, and involved some 50,000 allied troops. At this time, Foss was Adjutant to Major Onslow, the Commanding Officer of 2nd Bedfordshires. Obeying orders from the Brigade Commander, Onslow sent Foss forward to assess the situation after a failed attack on a German position by 'A' Company, during which 'every officer and man was hit, many as they left the trenches… those who made it into No Man's Land lay in a straight line where they fell'.

Charles Foss suggested that an attack by a bombing section could take the position, not mentioning that he intended to lead them! With a section of eight men from 'D' Company 'we then launched an attack. Words seem grand but we felt very "naked" and "above ground" - at least I did!' Having safely negotiated a flooded dyke, which they vaulted to avoid getting their feet wet, they 'threw a few bombs… The bombs, the first I had seen go off in anger, frightened me with their noise and the mess they made of the local Germans. They also stirred the Germans into activity - they got up and crowded round us with their hands up!' Captain Foss and his eight bombers captured an officer and 51 other German prisoners, to say nothing of those they had killed during their bombing raid. Sadly, five of the eight bombers were killed in the next few weeks. The scale of this battle can be gauged by the fact that no less than ten Victoria Crosses were awarded to those who took part, including one to a rifleman of the Garwhal Infantry in the Indian Army. Foss's citation says:

After the enemy had captured a part of one of our trenches, and our counter-attack, made with one officer and twenty men, having failed (all but two of the party being killed or wounded in the attempt), Captain Foss, on his own initiative, dashed forward with eight men, and under heavy fire attacked the enemy with grenades. He captured the position and the fifty two Germans who were occupying it. The capture of this position from the enemy was of the greatest importance, and the utmost bravery was displayed in essaying the task with so few men.

The tactical objective of the battle was to take control of Aubers Ridge above

Lille, which would have enabled the Allies to command operations around the town. The French were unable to fulfill their part of the planned action leaving the British lines insufficiently prepared for the event, and the result was that it was a failure with frightful casualties. Part of this attack was on Givenchy, carried out by some of the battalions of The King's Liverpool Regiment. In November 1915, the 18th Battalion of The King's (one of the Pal's Battalions) transferred to the 21st Brigade, and its place was taken by the 2nd Battalion of the Bedfords. In May 1915, Captain Foss again led a team of bombers at the Battle for Festubert but on 22 May was moved back to his post as Adjutant.

Captain Foss was later given the Brevets of Major and Lieutenant Colonel and from August 1915 served on the Staff as Brigade Major of the 20th Infantry Brigade, 7th Division; he was appointed GSO2 of the 1st and 2nd Canadian Divisions, and later of XXII Corps, and then as GSO1 of the 57th Division. He was Mentioned in Despatches on five occasions.

On 5 June 1915, he married Vere Katherine, widow of Captain Collard, of the 90th Punjabis, the third daughter of the late J. Lambert Ovans. She died in 1947, and in 1950 he married Phyllis Ruth, widow of Arthur Howie, of Ceylon.

In 1930, Colonel Charles C. Foss VC, DSO, came to The King's Liverpool Regiment (KLR) as Commanding Officer, after his long association with the 2nd Battalion of the Bedfordshire Regiment, remaining there until 1933 when he relinquished his command. It is this period of his military career which brings him within the scope of this book. Charles Foss succeeded Lieutenant Colonel L.R.Schuster in command of the 2nd Battalion and during his tenure in office, together with the Colonel of the Regiment, General Sir Charles Harington, he entertained King George V, who had become the Regiment's Colonel in Chief, in the Officers' Mess of the 2nd Battalion in Aldershot in 1932. In 1933, Charles Foss relinquished command of the Battalion, being succeeded by Lieutenant Colonel J.L. Short. During Foss's command, in 1931, the King's Regiment was given the freedom of the City of Liverpool with the privilege of marching through the City with colours flying and bayonets fixed.

From 1933 until 1937, Foss commanded the Rangoon Brigade Area, and during this time served also as ADC to King George VI. During the Second World War as Brigadier (Retired), he was involved with the Bedfordshire Local Defence Volunteers (later Home Guard), and was County Commandant of the Bedfordshire Army Cadet Force. He died in hospital in London on 9 April 1953, aged 68 years, and is buried in West Hill Cemetery, Winchester, Hampshire. His Victoria Cross and medal set are displayed in the Bedfordshire and Hertfordshire Regiment Museum in Luton.

$\mathcal{J}$an Edward Fraser
VC DSC

Born on 18 December 1920 at 79 Uxbridge Road, Baling, Middle-sex, Ian Edward Fraser was the son of Sydney and Florence Irene (née McKenzie). When he was six months old, Ian and his mother went out to Kuala Lumpur, Malaya, where his father was employed as a marine engineer. He returned to England to begin his schooling at Wallasey, Wirral, going on to the Royal Grammar School, High Wycombe, in Buckinghamshire. It was from here in 1936, that he enrolled as a cadet on the Mersey training ship HMS *Conway*. After completing his training he hoped to fulfil his ambition of joining the Royal Navy, but his application was unsuccessful.

Ian Edward Fraser VC DSC

In 1938, he entered the Merchant Navy as a Cadet Officer with the Blue Star Line, his first ship being the motor ship *Tuscan Star*, built in 1929, of almost 12,000 tons. His next ship was the *Sydney Star*, built in 1936, and on one voyage she was in a collision in Sydney Harbour, which kept Fraser there for six months while repairs were carried out. Although disappointed at not being accepted for the Navy, he had done the next best thing on joining the Merchant Service by becoming a cadet in the Royal Naval Reserve.

In June 1939, he was posted to the battleship HMS *Royal Oak* for what was supposed to be a four-month training exercise including a visit to Weymouth, in

Dorset, to take part in the 1939 Review of the Fleet. His training however, was interrupted with the outbreak of war on 3 September 1939, and it was not long before he joined the destroyer HMS *Keith*, the 'B' Class Flotilla Leader serving in the now hostile home waters. (The *Royal Oak* was torpedoed and sunk by German submarine U47 in October 1939, while *Keith* was sunk off Dunkirk during Operation Dynamo.) In the evacuation of Dunkirk (Operation Dynamo) in June 1940, Fraser was serving aboard the destroyer HMS *Montrose*, and continued in the destroyer service until late 1941, having in the summer of that year taken part in the destruction of U-651 in the Atlantic, while serving on HMS *Malcolm*.

Fraser volunteered for submarines, a decision that was obviously not at all influenced by the fate of the U-651, and he began training on the P35, and the smaller and much older H43. If any would-be submariners had any doubts on the wisdom of their decision to volunteer, these 23-year-old vessels were the ones to put it to the test! Completing his training on 10 April 1942 he was appointed Third Officer on the 'S' Class submarine HMS *Sahib*, which had been completed that year by the Cammell Laird yard. She had a complement of 44 officers and men, and belonged to the Tenth (Malta) Submarine Flotilla.

In April 1942 the island of Malta was awarded the George Cross for the courage of its inhabitants under constant air attack, for the Mediterranean was a theatre of continual war activity. As the Axis forces drove the Eighth Army back towards Egypt so it became necessary for them to increase their supplies and reinforcements from Italy to the North African ports. Their convoys were heavily guarded on the water and in the air and it was an extremely hazardous and dangerous proposition to attempt an attack in such circumstances. The Malta Submarine Flotilla however, made their presence felt with some significant successes, and their patrols continued throughout the year.

In the early part of 1943, a critical time because the enemy was fighting a desperate rearguard action in an attempt to retain control of the North African coast, the *Sahib* sought out and sank the U-301 as well as a number of supply ships, a critical time because the enemy was fighting a desperate rear-guard action in an attempt to retain control of the North African coast. It was this successful operation in the *Sahib* that led the *London Gazette* to announce on 6 April 1943 that Sub-Lieutenant Ian Fraser had been awarded the Distinguished Service Cross, ' For bravery and skill in successful submarine patrols '.

It is easy to imagine the real need to unwind and relax after having been on patrol and it was while at a wardroom celebration on the depot-ship that Fate played a hand in the life of Ian Fraser. During the party, there was some horseplay resulting in him breaking a metatarsal in his foot, which necessitated him being sent home on the cruiser HMS *Dido*. On 24 April HMS *Sahib* went out again on patrol without him and was depth-charged by an Italian destroyer in the vicinity of Cape Milazzo, Sicily. *Sahib* was scuttled by her crew and they were taken prisoner. It could well be that the party and his injury saved Fraser's life. *Dido* was another product of the Cammell Laird yard. As a tragic coincidence the Sahib had been scuttled and lost in the same area where, a month earlier on 13 March 1943, the submarine HMS *Thunderbolt* (formerly the ill-fated *Thetis*) was lost to depth charges.

After he had recovered from his injury, Fraser was sent to Northern Ireland, and having been promoted to Lieutenant was made First Officer on the H44, another of the old 1919 vessels used primarily for training. This was not the life he had been seeking, as he had been in action almost from the start of the war and felt that he should be doing something more useful. He volunteered for 'special and hazardous service', the precise meaning of which was unknown to him, but the speed by which his offer was accepted took him completely by surprise and almost before he knew it he was off to join the 12th Submarine Flotilla at Rothesay in Scotland. This was March 1944.

Here he became acquainted with the midget submarine. There was some doubt in his mind at first about being involved with manned torpedoes, a prospect that he did not relish as he hoped to continue in the submarine service. The newly developed 'X' craft offered the very adventure and daring for which he longed. They were submarines with a new potential and he was keen to be a part of it. First training began on the X20, in the waters of Loch Striven off the Kyle of Bute, their base being HMS *Varbell* at Port Bannatyne. Training in these small vessels had first started in 1942, and much had been learned and changed both in design and tactics during the following two years, but the principal features remained in that the craft was to be employed to carry some four tons of explosive in two special containers which straddled the hull. These would be released beneath the hull of an enemy vessel and detonated by a time fuse. They would in addition carry 'limpet' mines which could be magnetically attached to a ship's bottom. The 'X' craft was fitted with a 'wet and dry' compartment whereby a frogman, as a crew member, could leave the vessel and return while underwater.

Two midgets, X6 and X7, successfully entered Kaafiord, in Norway on 22 September 1943 and disabled the 42,000 ton battleship *Tirpitz*, and both commanders, Donald Campbell and Godfrey Place, were awarded the Victoria Cross. There were other successes but also tragic losses, some of them in training. It was obvious that this branch of the service was one of the most dangerous and called for men of special character.

A slightly larger craft was built to be used against the Japanese, known as 'XE' craft; Ian Fraser was appointed as commander of XE3. The vessel was just over 50 feet long, with a beam less than six feet, a height of seven feet, and weighed 30 tons. With diesel engine, fuel tanks, electric motors, batteries and all the necessary equipment including a toilet, and a crew of four, there was very little room to move, and for the most part of any time spent underwater it was very uncomfortable indeed.

A decision to move to the Far East had been taken and the XE craft were shipped out on the deck of their depot ship HMS *Bonaventure* (later to go back in service as the *Clan Davidson*). Their arrival in the South West Pacific was something of an anticlimax, for the controlling US Naval authorities were not impressed and it looked at first as if there was to be no action for the XEs. However, Captain Fell RN, the commander of the flotilla, was asked if it was possible to use such craft to cut the underwater telephone cables at Hong Kong and Saigon to interrupt the Japanese communications, and after trials this was agreed. At the same time it was suggested that two Japanese cruisers, each of 10,000 tons, and moored in the Johore Straits at Singapore, could be disabled. This gave the flotilla three active operations and so in July 1945 plans were put in hand to carry them through.

The two Japanese cruisers, *Takao* and *Myoko*, had been damaged previously in action and were lying in the Straits alongside Singapore naval dockyard awaiting repairs. It was believed that, although damaged, they could use their guns to some effect against the Allied land forces and cause considerable delays as well as casualties. The plan to deal with them was codenamed Operation Struggle.

The XE craft were transported to Labuan Island off the north-west coast of Borneo, and from there on 26 July 1945 they set off on their epic journey of 650 miles to the Straits of Singapore. Lieutenant J.E. Smart RNVR, was in command of XE1, and XE3 was under the command of Lieutenant Ian Fraser DSC RNR. The midget craft were towed by the 'S' class submarines HMS *Spark* and HMS *Stygian* respectively. They travelled on the surface during the night and were submerged during the day. The XE vessels were manned by 'passage' crews for this part of the journey while the operational crews were aboard the towing submarines. After four days, in the early hours of 30 July, the operational crews took over their vessels, and one can imagine from this point the tension felt by each individual as they changed over. The four submarines moved off, again submerged, and just after 2300 hrs that night surfaced in the eastern approaches of the Straits where the tows were slipped and the two small craft went off towards their objectives alone. The *Spark* and *Stygian* were to rendezvous some 48 hours later.

The XE1 had been given the *Myoko* as its target and as she was a little further up the Straits than the *Takao* she moved ahead, with the XE3 a few miles behind. Both commanders were entirely alone in their endeavours now and unfortunately the XE1 encountered a number of ships, which slowed her progress down so much that she would not have been able to reach her target and return in time. Meanwhile, Fraser took his vessel on towards the Johore Straits with the intention of being able to survey the boom across the entrance by periscope just as dawn was about to break. Fortunately, the boom was open to allow the passage of an enemy ship and they daringly went through with the enemy vessel almost alongside while they were just below the surface. Again their luck held out and they were not spotted by any of the crew on the deck of the ship.

Fraser's crew comprised Lieutenant W.J.L. Smith RNVR, a New Zealander; Engine-room Artificer C.A. Read and Acting Leading Seaman J.J. Magennis, all experienced submariners. They encountered significant shipping in the Johore Strait and this made their task all the more arduous as they tried to maintain speed unobserved so that they could carry out their task when the tide was high. Inside the little XE submarine it was most uncomfortable; apart from being tense and cramped, the temperature was almost unbearable and signs of exhaustion were now beginning to show.

At 1250 hrs, Fraser spotted *Takao*, and later said that 'although she seemed to appear with the suddenness of an apparition, I had the feeling I had been staring at her for a long time. She was very heavily camouflaged and she lay in the exact position I had plotted on my chart'. The cruiser appeared to be aground at the bows and stern with an area of deep water amidships, and it was to this area of water that the XE craft was manoeuvred for the attack. It was not possible to gauge the position easily for the water was so clear and they had been forced suddenly out of line in order to avoid a collision with a motor cutter laden with Japanese soldiers as it passed over the top of them. In diving quickly they grounded on the bottom and then, rising, they hit the cruiser hard and too far forward so that further manoeuvring was needed. It was now 1500 hrs and they had been without sleep for 20 hours and submerged for half that time. Jim Magennis had donned his frogman's suit and made his way outside working at the barnacle encrusted hull of the enemy vessel to fix his limpet mines. He worked hard and diligently while the other crew members sweated, anxiously awaiting his return. It was 1600 hrs before he returned, utterly exhausted, his hands torn by the sharp barnacles.

They took off his frogman's suit and gave him a drink. Fraser gave the order to release the two side charges, each containing two tons of Amatol with their timing clocks set for 2130 hrs. The port charge fell away cleanly but the limpet carrier above the starboard charge was jammed against the hull of the cruiser. The XE3 was trapped by her own charge and the immediate prospect appeared that the submariners would be blown up. Fraser prepared to go outside to try to release the vessel from its predicament, but Magennis, now somewhat recovered, insisted that he was the frogman and it was his job to do it. Reluctantly, Fraser agreed. He had great confidence in his crew and knew that Magennis was capable of doing the right thing. The frogman climbed out with some difficulty owing to the tilted position of the craft and armed with a large spanner began to free the carrier above the charge. It seemed an eternity as the three men inside the submarine silently awaited the return of their colleague. It was not long before Magennis forced himself back into the wet and dry chamber, and the starboard charge then dropped clear. Relief is too inadequate a word to express the feelings of those on board as Fraser restored the composure of his crew and made headway into the Straits. A tricky journey faced them before they reached the open sea but they successfully cleared the boom and at 0330 hrs they were taken in tow by the *Stygian*.

The XE1, unable to reach its objective, moved in on the *Takao* after XE3 and without attempting to move under the cruiser dropped her side charges alongside and then made haste to clear the boom before it closed. They were collected by the submarine *Spark*. The four vessels then made the long journey back to Labuan, their mission carried out in the best traditions of the Service. Lieutenant Ian Fraser and Leading Seaman James Magennis were each awarded the Victoria Cross; Lieutenant Smith was awarded the Distinguished Service Order; and Engine-Room Artificer Read was awarded the Conspicuous Gallantry Medal.

Later it was found that the *Takao* had only a skeleton crew on board which was probably why the XE3 had gone unnoticed. The cruiser had been almost written off by the Japanese and the result of the explosive charges only served to confirm this for they blew a huge hole in the bottom of the ship rendering it useless. However, although with hindsight the mission turned out to be somewhat unnecessary, there had been plans to return the XE's to repeat the task after they arrived aboard HMS *Bonaventure*. The operation was a success in many ways, and it was mainly through their skill and courage that the two crews of the midgets had proved without doubt that the 'X' craft were a capable force for such activities.

On 11 December 1945, Lieutenant Ian Fraser DSC, RNR, received his Victoria Cross from King George VI at Buckingham Palace. It had been his hope to transfer to the Royal Navy after the war, but with so many regular officers available he did not pursue the matter and was discharged from the Service on 4 March 1947.

In 1943, while awaiting the refitting of the submarine H4 at Sheerness, he had married Melba Estelle Hughes, whom he had known in Wallasey for a number of years. She was a member of the WRNS and was stationed at Pwllheli on the North Wales coast. On 27 November 1944, Mrs. Fraser launched the XE3 at Rothesay, the vessel being given the unofficial name of *Sygin*, after the loving wife of the discordant Loki in Norse mythology. Fraser became the first married officer allowed to join the 'X' craft flotilla. They set up home in Wallasey and had a family of two daughters and four sons. Their eldest child was born six weeks before the *Takao* operation.

On 7 February 1946 Fraser attended a meeting of Wallasey Council with his wife and he was presented with a commemorative sword of honour by the Mayor (Alderman W.B. Millward). Mrs. Fraser received a gold Naval coronet brooch as a personal souvenir. Tributes were paid by the Mayor and leaders of the various groups on the Council, and a public subscription was opened so that local people could show their appreciation.

Leaving the Service in 1947 posed quite a few problems for the man who had spent those tense and anxious hours in the Strait of Johore, and he hoped his experience of working underwater in the Royal Navy could be developed for commercial purposes. He did not envisage however, the course he would have to take to bring this to reality. Today we know it is comparatively easy to start a business, and there are a number of practical and financial aids to help. In 1947, there was no such assistance and Fraser's resourcefulness led him in a most unlikely direction to achieve his objective. He joined a circus and, using his Victoria Cross as an added attraction, formed a group of underwater performers who carried out the role of frogmen in a mock-up of the 'X' craft action in a huge 20,000-gallon tank. This caused a few eyebrows to be raised among the Naval brass-hats, but Ian Fraser needed to raise some capital to start his own underwater business, and this novel if offbeat method gave him and his colleagues the means to do this.

The business was called Universal Divers Limited, and had an office at 40 North John Street, Liverpool, specialising in underwater surveys, repairs, construction and civil engineering, and using standard divers and frogmen. From small jobs such as removing obstructions, clearing debris and the like from the bottom of docks and lakes, the firm developed its expertise to meet the growing demands as the aftermath of the war saw a great deal of new construction taking place not only in this country but in other parts of the world. Under Fraser's able direction, Universal Divers Ltd. became the foremost diving company in the UK, and its reputation enabled it to undertake work anywhere. In the early years work was difficult to come by: civil engineering requirements, surveying and salvage methods, and the improvements and changes in welding techniques all had to be learned, keeping Fraser and his men busy. Early on, they were fortunate in acquiring some equipment from Sir Robert Davies, the eminent diving inventor and head of the Siebe, Gorman Company which was the principal supplier of conventional and frogman diving gear as well as other safety equipment. Sir Robert, who developed the Davies escape apparatus for the safety of submariners, was most impressed by Ian Fraser's efforts to get started. They also bought some equipment from the Liverpool & Glasgow Salvage Association when it closed down its depot in Liverpool.

The need for oil brought about dramatic changes, with off-shore drilling rigs and ancillary platforms requiring highly specialised diving companies to carry out underwater work. Bahrain, Nigeria, and the North Sea all beckoned and Universal Divers responded, so that the firm that was almost born in a circus was now leading the way in new technology and was the leading British company in underwater construction know-how. Ian Fraser VC, DSC had achieved his ambition. As Managing Director and then as Chairman he guided the company with the same meticulous care he had shown in the epic voyage of XE3 in the dangerous waters of the Johore Straits. In 1975 this successful company was sold to Star Offshore Services of Aberdeen, a move designed to ensure its future in further North Sea Oil development, and from that time until 1982 Ian Fraser remained a director of the larger concern. He retired in 1982.

A Justice of the Peace in Wallasey, he was also a life member of Leasowe Golf Club, New Brighton Rugby Union Football Club, and of Hoylake Sailing Club, the latter being a pastime he thoroughly enjoyed as he kept his contact with the sea. He also liked ship-modeling and this required a steady hand and much patience, attributes the great man still possessed even in old age. He was Vice-President of the Merseyside Branch of the Submariner's Old Comrades Association and a patron of the *Conway* Club.

Fraser also held the Legion of Merit, awarded in 1945 by the government of the United States of America. He was the last surviving recipient of the Victoria Cross on Merseyside, and in July 2007 played his part in a walk by Jack Moran, a 78-year-old himself, as part of the project to erect a memorial to Captain Noel Chavasse VC & Bar MC and fifteen Liverpool-born Victoria Cross winners. The walk was from Crosby to the Holocaust Memorial in Birkenhead, and Fraser was one half of a welcoming committee when Jack arrived at his destination; the other half was Arthur Dodd, a POW survivor from Auschwitz whose heroic tale is another story!

Fraser was himself a keen supporter of the Noel Chavasse Memorial project and in August 2008 it was hoped that he would unveil the memorial when it was finally erected in Abercromby Square, Liverpool. Sadly, Ian was taken ill a week or two prior to the unveiling and was unable to attend the unveiling on 17 August. Three weeks later, he passed away. A Service of Thanksgiving on the day of his cremation, held at St James's Church, New Brighton, was attended by a great number of his friends and admirers, including members of the Submariners Association, and fittingly featured the hymns 'Eternal Father, Strong to Save' and 'Sunset and Evening Star'. To commemorate Ian Fraser, a limited edition lapel badge was commissioned and made available to all those

Ian Edward Fraser VC DSC

who attended the Service of Thanksgiving. The badge is in the form of a miniature Victoria Cross and the design signifies the fact that Ian was the last surviving member of the 14 submariners and the 119 Royal Naval personnel who received the award. Only 119 badges were produced, with Number 1 going to Ian's widow, Melba, and Number 119 to the Rear Admiral Submarines.

Ian Fraser was a gentle man, a gentleman and a thoroughly nice person. The Noel Chavasse VC Memorial Association is now planning to include him on the plinth of their VC Memorial to 'Liverpool Heroes'. His Victoria Cross is part of Lord Ashcroft's collection.

George Ward Gunn
VC MC

George Ward Gunn VC MC

Born on 26 July 1912 at Muggleswick, County Durham, on the border with Northumberland, George Ward Gunn was the eldest of four sons born to George Gunn and Grace née Ritson. The family settled in Church Road, Neston, Wirral, where George (Senior) became the local doctor. Young George went to school at Mostyn House, Parkgate, an independent private school founded and run by the Grenfell family since 1854. The school was originally in Tarvin but was resited in 1855 in the Mostyn Arms, formerly the 18th Century George Inn. Mostyn House School has an unusual memorial to its 80 or so former pupils who lost their lives in the Great War, in the form of a carillon of 31 bells over its chapel. Later, George and his three brothers went to Sedbergh School, an independent boarding school in Yorkshire established in 1525. After school, George became a chartered accountant and Company Secretary with Messrs Sissons & Co. Ltd. of London.

On the first day of the Second World War he volunteered for the Royal Artillery as a gunner and was called up in December 1939. In August 1940 he was granted a commission as Second Lieutenant in the Royal Regiment of Artillery and was posted to the 3rd Regiment Royal Horse Artillery. Shortly afterwards he was serving in the Middle East as part of the 7th Armoured

Brigade in the Eighth Army. In beleaguered Tobruk in January 1941 he earned the Military Cross, for 'sustained gallantry and coolness which inspired all ranks under heavy and close enemy fire on a number of occasions, and particularly on January 4th and 5th, as one of the heroic Tobruk garrison'. This award appeared in the *London Gazette* of 6 May 1941.

At this time Rommel and his Afrika Corps were holding the upper hand in their advance across Libya. They had isolated the port of Tobruk where British and Commonwealth forces were besieged, and had then swept on beyond towards the Egyptian border. Their progress, however, was not as rapid as it might sound, nor was it completely to Rommel's liking, for there was a great deal of stubborn resistance for the Germans to overcome at a great cost to both sides in men and equipment. On 18 November 1941 the Allies launched an offensive codenamed Operation Crusader, and the Eighth Army made consistent and rapid progress with the aim of destroying the Axis Forces in Cyrenaica, occupy Tripolitania and drive the Germans out of Africa, in order to relieve Tobruk. By 20 November, 7th Armoured Division had overrun the airfield at Sidi Rezegh but then found their route towards Tobruk blocked by German infantry and anti-tank guns. Reinforcements in the form of the Divisional Support Group under the command of Brigadier John ('Jock') Campbell arrived that evening, by which time the Germans had counter-attacked, leading to a confusing yet ferocious tank and anti-tank battle. Initially, Rommel used his 15th :Panzer Division to attack the 4th Armoured Brigade, while Campbell and the 7th Armoured Brigade held onto the airfield. Rommel realised that Operation Crusader was intended to drive his forces from Cyrenaica and decided to delay his assault on Tobruk and concentrate his resources on the important target of Sidi Rezegh airfield.

At dawn on 21 November, he launched a major panzer attack, taking the Allies by surprise. The 7th Hussars were all but wiped out by 21st Panzer, while 15th Panzer destroyed the tanks of 2nd Royal Tank Regiment. The 1st King's Royal Rifle Corps, with 2nd Rifle Brigade and 6th Royal Tank Regiment launched an attack on the Sidi Rezegh ridge, taking a terrible beating but eventually taking the ridge. In their subsequent defence of the ridge, Rifleman John Beeley, KRRC was awarded the Victoria Cross.

The full force of the German armour was now aimed at the 7th Armoured Brigade and the Support Group to the south of the airfield. That afternoon, some 50 German tanks attacked, driving over the gentle rise to the east of the Sidi

Rezegh saucer, but at the head of the incline were brought to a surprised halt by the 25-pounders of the 60th Field Regiment RA, and the little two-pounders on their portees of two troops of 'J' Battery, 3rd R.H.A. These were C Troop, under Lieutenant Hardy and A Troop under George Gunn. (A Portee was a carrying vehicle on which guns were transported; 'en portee' was when the guns were actually fired from the carrying trucks instead of from the ground.) Four German tanks went up in flames and the rest turned tail. This was the precursor of the great battle to follow.

Rommel decided to concentrate his Panzer attack against the airfield and at dawn on 21 November 1941 launched a major Panzer attack; a powerful force of some 60 German tanks in the first wave accompanied by flights of Stuka Divebombers moved towards the Sidi Rezegh positions of the British support group. At the same time the German artillery laid down a barrage across the British line. The tanks were fearlessly engaged by the comparatively minute firepower of the British artillery and before long six tanks were disabled. This brought an additional and very heavy response from the enemy artillery erupting in a deafening clamour of more than two hundred guns, enveloped in smoke and dust, streaked with tracers of shot and bullet, stabbed by the flashes of guns of both sides, inflamed by burning trucks and ammunition. Never before had the Afrika Corps had such a reception from what seemed easy prey. The British guns held their ground, although completely exposed and their casualties mounting.

At the southern end of the battle lay A Troop under George Ward Gunn. They had been firing away but the range was too long for the two-pounder to have a positive killing effect, so with extraordinary daring he moved his guns right forward in the open to close the range. The enemy responded with ferocity, but the gunners carried out their duties undaunted, and as their casualties mounted so the survivors moved to other guns to make the teams up. George Gunn, riding in a small open truck, darted from gun to gun, manoeuvring them to get the best advantage and encouraged his men as he directed their fire. Eventually there were only two guns left in action and these were subjected to heavy fire. Their crews were killed or wounded except for a Sergeant Grey. When one of these two remaining guns was destroyed, Gunn dashed through the flames of the blazing portee of the remaining gun and with Grey acting as loader and with the help of the Battery Commander, Major Pinney, Gunn fired off 40 or 50 rounds. In spite of their critical situation with fire all around and the ammunition at risk, his accuracy at a range of about 800 yards was unerring, and at least two enemy tanks were disabled and others damaged before he fell dead, shot through the forehead.

George Gunn showed the most conspicuous courage in attacking such a large number of tanks with a single unarmoured gun, and his utter disregard for extreme danger was an example which inspired all who saw it. He remained undismayed by intense fire and overwhelming odds, and his gallant resistance only ceased with his death. But for his very gallant action the enemy tanks would undoubtedly have overrun the Allied position.

Gunn was awarded the Victoria Cross posthumously, and is buried in Knightsbridge War Cemetery, Acroma, Libya. There is a memorial to him in the church of St. Mary and St. Helen, in Neston, where there is also a plaque, placed there in 1964 following the closure of Neston Memorial Cottage Hospital where it had featured near a bed endowed in his memory by friends.

The 7th Armoured Division won three VCs at Sidi Rezegh on 21 November 1941. In addition to George Gunn, VCs were awarded to Brigadier John 'Jock' Campbell DSO MC, Royal Horse Artillery and also to Private John Beeley, King's Royal Rifle Corps. Beeley's award, like that of George Gunn, was posthumous. Brigadier Campbell survived the action but died in a car crash in 1942. Campbell, by a strange coincidence, was also an Old Boy of Sedbergh School. The school has a Combined Cadet Force which began in 1901 as the Sedbergh School Rifle Corps and can boast a total of four VC winners: Jock Campbell, George Gunn, Kenneth Campbell (RAF) and Robert Digby-Jones (Royal Engineers). George Gunn had three younger brothers, one of whom served with the Royal Artillery, another with the Royal Army Medical Corps, while the third was a medical student during the Great War. All four attended Sedbergh School, where they are said to have been collectively known as the 'Gunn Battery'!

Gunn's appearance and general demeanour was not that of a hardened hero. A man of slight build, good looking, with dark hair and a dark upturned moustache in the fashion of the age of the 'flappers', he did however look like a soldier, with a charming and attractive personality, full of gay spirit but firm of purpose. He showed the panache of the 'horse-gunner', wearing a blue scarf and the red, blue and gold regimental mess cap of the Royal Artillery instead of a khaki one. How deceptive can appearances be! Whenever he was in action he worked as hard as anyone, and his determination in critical times was admired by all who served with him. He never married and his Victoria Cross is displayed in the Royal Artillery Museum, Woolwich.

(The Church of St Mary and St Helen in Neston also has a memorial to Merseyside VC winner Christopher Bushell VC DSO; see page 15 in this volume).

*H*arry Hampton VC

Harry Hampton VC

Born on 14 December 1871 at 1 Sheen Dale, Richmond, Surrey, the son of Samuel Hampton, a carpenter, and of Mary (née Inglefield), Harry Hampton's early life is something of an unknown quantity. We do know that in the 1881 Census the family, with its 8 children, is shown as living at 17 Crown Terrace, Richmond. We also know that Harry enlisted in the 1st Battalion of the King's Liverpool Regiment (KLR) at Aldershot on 10 March 1889 when he gave his age as 18 years and 2 months and his occupation as 'Butcher'. He signed on initially for 7 years Regular and 5 years Reserve Service but subsequently extended this, eventually serving for 21 years. His papers indicate that on enlistment he was only 5'4" tall with a 33" chest, yet weighing 12 stone. His education in civilian life is unknown except that there is a suggestion in his file that he may have spent some time in an Industrial School, but we know that whilst serving he received some education at Military School and obtained his Army 3rd Class and the 2nd Class Certificates of Education in June 1889 and 1890 respectively.

His service record shows that after initial training and home service between 11.03.1889 and 09.02.1891, he served in Bermuda (10.02.1891 to 19.03.1893); Halifax, Nova Scotia (20.03.1893 to 06.12.1895); Barbados (07.12.1895 to

06.11.1897); South Africa (07.11.1897 to 28.10.1900); home (23.10.1900 to 16.03.1906); and St Lucia (17.03.1906 to 10.03.1910). He was promoted Corporal two years later on 10 February 1891 and Sergeant on 27 April 1895. As war against the Boers began to appear inevitable, the 1st KLR formed a company of mounted infantry and moved to Ladysmith for intensive training, and Harry Hampton became a mounted infantryman. Early defeats when the 2nd Boer War broke out in 1899, including the sieges of Kimberley and Mafeking, were followed by a prolonged siege of Ladysmith, into which township the British had been obliged to retreat.

Harry Hampton was amongst those members of his Regiment who were sent to assist the defenders of Wagon Hill against a Boer attack on 6 January 1900 and were under very heavy shell and rifle fire all day. The siege of Ladysmith was to last over 4 months, relief not arriving until 28 February 1900, by which time the garrison had been reduced to eating its own horses and mules. After the siege, as part of the 4th Division Mounted Infantry, he took part in the advance through Natal and the Eastern Transvaal and was almost continually engaged with the enemy.

On 21 August 1900, at Van Wyk's Vlei, his unit was opposed by a numerically much superior force of Boers and the troopers were only able to withdraw from the position they had taken up through the cool and gallant conduct of Sergeant Hampton and Corporal Henry James Knight (see later at page 69). Sergeant Harry Hampton was in command of a small detached party of Mounted Infantry. When he saw his men being driven back by the much larger force of Boers, he held onto his position, a most important one, for some considerable time against greater numbers. When he found that his position was untenable and they were compelled to retire, the withdrawal was carried out in a most skilful manner. Hampton saw all his men to safety, and although wounded in the head, he supported Lance Corporal Walsh who was badly wounded and unable to walk, until Walsh was hit again by a bullet and killed. Harry Hampton was also wounded rather severely shortly afterwards and his army records show that he was wounded in the head, right thigh and right leg.

For this act of gallantry, Harry Hampton was awarded the Victoria Cross, one of three won by the King's Liverpool Regiment in as many days, the others being Knight and William Edward Heaton. Hampton was decorated with his medal by King Edward VII, at St. James's Palace, London on 17 December 1901. His father, Samuel, now 75 years old, was in 1901 still living at 17 Crown

Terrace, a widower but having a number of boarders. It is nice to think that he may have been present on his son's great day.

Harry was promoted to Colour Sergeant, and then in 1906 became Sergeant Instructor in Musketry with the St Lucia Police. He was discharged in March 1910 after completing 21 years' service, his conduct being described as exemplary, and intending on discharge to continue to live on St Lucia. However, he joined the Corps of Commissionaires in London on 11 December 1912, and was employed for some time at the Society of Architects Club, and at the Builder's Exhibition at Olympia in 1920.

Hampton died on 2 November 1922, from shock following a fractured skull and injury to his leg caused by being accidentally struck by a train at St. Margaret's Station, London. The inquest heard that a short time previously, when he was alighting from an omnibus, his leg had given way and he had fallen, fracturing his thigh. It is thought that his leg had again caused him to fall when walking along the station platform. At the time of his death, he was living at 151 Halliburton Road, Isleworth.

Hampton's Army Record shows that he had married Gertrude Lythgoe on 27 February 1906 in Warrington, shortly before he was posted to St Lucia. They had at least one daughter, Elsie Florence Gertrude, born on 8 July 1908 in St Lucia. It has been suggested that he may have committed suicide at the railway station, and it has been claimed in a newspaper cutting of 13 March 1986 that his wife burned his Victoria Cross in her distress at his suicide. Another newspaper report at the time of the inquest in 1922 states that he was wearing his medal when he fell but it was missing afterwards and his relatives were seeking its return. In fact, his VC was until recently part of the King's Liverpool display in the Museum of Liverpool Life, Liverpool. The display has gone into storage pending the construction of a new Museum and no doubt will then again be displayed, along with those of William Heaton, Henry Knight and David Jones.

In 1986, Police Constable Ron Biddle, of the Metropolitan Police, whose hobby was tracing the graves of holders of the Victoria Cross, found the grave of Sergeant Harry Hampton VC, unmarked and neglected in the Richmond Cemetery Old Burial Ground. It had taken him months to find it, and it is almost incredible to hear that his burial place was unknown to his family for more than 60 years. PC Biddle contacted the King's Regimental Secretary, and later an inscribed headstone was erected and dedicated in a touching ceremony attended by his last surviving relatives. Colonel Sir Geoffrey Errington read out his citation and Lieutenant Colonel Jeremy Gaskell, the Regiment's Commanding Officer, was also present. A photograph of the headstone shows that the inscription gives his date of death as February 1920, which is inconsistent with the date on his death certificate, and with the newspaper accounts of the time. We know that Harry Hampton attended a Garden Party at Buckingham Palace in June 1920, and his signature appears on a menu card signed by those present.

The standard work on the Victoria Cross by General Sir 0'Moore Creagh and Miss Humphris gives Hampton's birthplace as Crown Terrace, Richmond, as does his Army record, and his date of birth as 14 December 1870. Sid Lindsay had a copy of his birth certificate, which confirmed the details given at the beginning of this article and it would be a strange coincidence if there were two Harry Hamptons born on the same date but 12 months apart, whose fathers were both named Samuel. Finally, on 23 February 2005, an AA mechanic answered a call to a broken down car on the M3 Motorway and was delighted to find that the driver was the great-grandson of Harry Hampton, presumably still living in the south east.

Henry James Knight VC

Henry James Knight VC

K night was born on 5 November 1878 at Park Street, Yeovil, Somerset, and was christened James Huntley Knight, son of the late Huntley Knight and Alma (née Hann). His father was employed as a cloth weaver, a minor industry in those parts manufacturing high quality material, but died in spring 1878, and the loss of his father before Henry was born must have placed the family in rather dire circumstances. In fact the 1881 Census shows Henry living with his maternal grandparents, George and Hannah Hann, in Yeovil, while the only Alma Knight is shown as a boarder with a family named Allway in Poole St James, Dorset. (There is nothing to say that this is Henry's mother). In the 1891 Census there is a James Knight, about the right age and born in Yeovil, living as an 'inmate' in an industrial school at Milborne Stileham, Blandford in Dorset. Again, there is nothing to confirm that this is Henry James Knight although it seems likely in view of the final paragraph of this chapter. In truth, it has proved impossible to find any details of Henry's early life. Sid Lindsay tried the King's Regiment, the London Scottish, the Royal British Legion and even spoke to members of Knight's family – none was able or prepared to help. It seems reasonable to assume that he enlisted as soon as he was of age, joining the 1st Battalion of the King's (Liverpool) Regiment (KLR) using the name Henry James Knight.

In the South African War, at the age of 22, Knight made his mark on British military history. On 21 August 1900, as a Corporal in No 1 Mounted Infantry belonging to the 1st Bn KLR during operations near Van Wyks Vlie, Corporal Knight was deployed in some rocks with four men, covering the right rear of a detachment of the same Company, who, under Captain Ewart, were holding the right of the line. The enemy, about 50 strong, attacked Ewart 's right and almost surrounded at short range Corporal Knight's small party. Knight's citation states that he, a non-commissioned officer, held his ground, directing his party to retire one by one to better cover, while he maintained his position for over an hour, covering the withdrawal of Captain Ewart's force, and losing two of his four men. He then retired, bringing with him two wounded men. One of these he left in a place of safety, the other he carried for nearly two miles. He and his party were hotly engaged during the whole time. (Note: on 29 January 1906 Captain F.R.Ewart, KLR, was awarded the Royal Humane Society's bronze medal for diving fully clothed into a lagoon at Lagos and rescuing a native boy who had fallen in. At the time, Captain Ewart was serving with the Lagos Battalion in the West African Frontier Force.) Knight was promoted Sergeant, and was presented with his Victoria Cross by General Lord Kitchener of Khartoum, GCB, at Pretoria, Transvaal, on 8 June 1902.

Although he rose to the rank of Colour Sergeant, little is known of Knight's Army service other than that in 1915 it was stated that he had been a Sergeant Major and Quartermaster Sergeant in the 'Empire Battalion'. This unit was formed on 31 August 1914 by a body of military and businessmen in London who supported the British Empire Committee. The Empire Battalion was to become the 17th Battalion of the Royal Fusiliers and played an active role in France from November 1915. The website of the Royal Fusiliers 1914-1918 shows that Captain W.N.Stone, whilst a member of 17th Battalion, was awarded a Victoria Cross at Moeuvres near Cambrai on 30 November 1917, although the VC *Register* says he was in the 3rd Battalion.

It is not known whether Knight was with the 1st King's when the 1914 War started, or if he was a member of the British Expeditionary Force, or if he was at Mons, although this is unlikely if he served in the Empire Battalion. In February 1915 he was granted a commission and appointed to the 20th (5th City) Battalion The Manchester Regiment. In March 1915 he was promoted to Temporary Captain in that battalion.

In May 1915, the Empire Battalion attracted adverse attention with reports of a scandal involving contracts to civilians for work and services at the Battalion's camp, in which it was claimed that illicit payments had been made. The Commanding Officer, Lieutenant Colonel Bowden, was also a serving Member of Parliament, and these issues were raised in the House of Commons. A Court of Inquiry was set up, and no less a legal personage than Major Sir. F.E. Smith, of the Judge Advocates Department took part. (Smith was later to become the Attorney General and was elevated to the peerage as Lord Birkenhead.)

Captain Knight was called to give evidence, having held a responsible position in the Empire Battalion as quartermaster. In that capacity he would have had some dealings with the contractors but only in the manner in which they did their work. During the course of his evidence, Knight made the observation that as far as the catering was concerned, 'the food was never insufficient, but it was badly cooked, as the authorities appointed a master cook who did not know his work, and might have been a bricklayer'. He went on to tell the Court about the condition of the men's huts, saying that the inspecting officers never went to the huts when they were leaking, and that men had been seen floating paper boats in the water inside the huts.

His evidence was probably mostly true, but it was not accepted by the Court, and he earned a rebuke from Major Sir F.E. Smith. Captain Knight then withdrew his remarks.

The Inquiry went on until August, and although the principal civilians and the Commanding Officer appeared from time to time to be close to criminal prosecution, in the end nothing came of the affair, and in December 1915 it was announced in the House of Commons that no charges would be laid. Nevertheless, something happened to Knight, because in October 1915 he relinquished his commission, no reason being given. The matter was not reported in the Press, but to add to the mystery, on the front page of the *Daily Mirror* on 17 November 1915 there was a picture of Henry James Knight VC under the caption 'Ex-Sergeant-Major joins the London Scottish as a Private'.

He was later promoted to Corporal and was wounded in July 1916 at Gommecourt, during the Battle of the Somme. This attack took place on 1 July 1916, the first day of the battle, and was intended to draw some of the German reserves away from the main offensive further south but also attracted the attention of German artillery. Initial successes were quickly stalled, with many casualties before the British were obliged to withdraw.

Little is known of the later life of this heroic man other than that he attended a VC Reunion Dinner at the House of Lords on 9 November 1929 and died on 24 November 1955, aged 76 years, at Winterborne Anderson; he was cremated at Bournemouth Crematorium. Milbourne St Andrew, or more properly Milbourne St Andrew with Milbourne Stileham, is a village situated some 12 miles from Poole in Dorset. In 1857 the Dorset Boys Industrial School was opened in the village and in 1891 the population of Milbourne St Andrew was 286 whilst that of Milbourne Stileham was 272, of whom 75 were pupils or inmates of the industrial school. Here, the boys were trained for a career in agriculture, tailoring, shoemaking, baking, the sea and the army, so perhaps this was how Knight came to enlist. His Victoria Cross is in the possession of the King's Regimental Museum in Liverpool.

John Simpson Knox
VC

John Simpson Knox was born on 30 September 1828 at King Street, Calton, Glasgow, the son of John Knox and his second wife Rebekah (née Living). (John Knox's first wife was Gliten Marshall, whom he married in 1805, but the date of her death is not known, and he remarried in 1826. He had been born in Inverkeithing, Fifeshire, and served for eight years in the 90th Light Infantry (Perthshire Volunteers) until 1802, then joining the 28th Regiment, Stirlingshire Militia, under the Duke of Montrose. Whilst serving with the 90th, he had learned how to dispense and make medical compounds and after working as a labourer became a grocer. He served eleven years with the Militia gaining the rank of Sergeant).

John Simpson Knox VC

John Simpson Knox had a very unhappy life at home, so much so that he ran away at the age of fourteen, and being very tall for his age enlisted in the Scots Fusilier Guards, at Glasgow, on 15 May 1843. It is said that he was bought out of the army but re-enlisted shortly afterwards. He was given the rank of Corporal in 1846, became a Sergeant in 1851; some ten years after his enlistment the Scots Fusilier Guards embarked for the Crimea. They landed on that gruesome peninsula on 14 September 1854 and four days later J.S. Knox was promoted to Colour Sergeant and marched off towards Sebastopol. On 19 September they had their first taste of action when they ran across enemy troops who had fired a village. There followed a sharp engagement in which the Scots

Guards routed their foe with fixed bayonets.

On 20 September, the British and French troops had reached the banks of the Alma River which carved its way through the undulating grass plain resembling a great amphitheatre banked by steep heights rising to almost 300 feet. In the deep ravines running down from the heights to the river, the Russians had strategically placed a number of pieces of artillery, with more heavy artillery on top of the heights supporting some 40,000 of their best troops. The French Chasseurs led the Allied advance and soon the Russian troops opened up with very heavy fire from cannon and musket onto the forces below. Although the guns of the Allied artillery inflicted many casualties among the enemy, they were unable to see the Russians but were in the clear view of the enemy themselves. The Scots Guards and other British units distinguished themselves in driving the enemy off the heights and into retreat, but at one stage in the battle there was some serious confusion caused by poor communications. The troops at the front of the attack had suffered tremendous casualties from the enemy bombardment and were ordered to retire through the lines to recover. This was interpreted by many as a general withdrawal and it was in these circumstances that John Simpson Knox became prominent, going forward under terrific enemy fire and rallying the men to advance as originally ordered and let the survivors pass behind safely. It was largely as a result of his intervention that the battle continued and a number of enemy batteries were captured. His fellow NCOs, seeing his lead, helped to rally the hard pressed troops when it looked as if the struggling officers might lose control. With the heights in Allied hands, the battle of Alma had been won. Sadly, the victory could have been more decisive if the commanders of the British and French forces had realised that to have pursued the retreating Russians could very well have brought the Crimean War to an end. The opportunity was missed.

In November 1854 the Allies moved on to Sebastopol, but not before they had defeated Russian counter-attacks at Balaclava (with the ill-conceived but heroic charge of the Light Brigade), and on 5 November the battle of Mount Inkerman where, after ten desperate hours of close fighting, the Russians were defeated. Once again the Scots Guards had demonstrated their fighting capacity and in particular the determination of Sergeant Knox to motivate and raise the morale of his men despite the terrible conditions in which they found themselves. Cholera and dysentery were rife, with almost non-existent medical services in the field. This and the cold, wet weather added to the hazards of battle. Knox claimed that he was insensitive to the terrors of battle, a view not shared by many, and at Sebastopol he was to prove himself a tough nut to crack.

The performance of the Guards at Inkerman so impressed HRH the Prince Consort that he offered a commission in his own regiment, The Rifle Brigade, to be selected by Major General Lord Rokeby, himself a veteran of Waterloo. Rokeby nominated Knox of the Scots Guards, while two other commissions went to the Grenadiers and Coldstream respectively. Lord Rokeby stated that he had witnessed the gallantry displayed by Knox since they had been in action and was extremely impressed by his devotion to duty beyond his rank. So Knox transferred from the Scots Guards to the Rifle Brigade with the rank of Lieutenant in April 1855, his appointment being backdated to 29 December 1854.

In June 1855, after a number of prolonged artillery bombardments of the now besieged Sebastopol, an attack by the Allied infantry was attempted, but despite the very considerable damage to the fortress town, and heavy casualties sustained by the Russians, the British attack was repulsed. It was during this attack that Knox, leading one of the Rifle Brigade ladder parties, came under devastating fire from the walls of the Redan. The Company Commander, Captain Blackett, had been severely wounded as had a great many men, and Knox took charge of the remainder. It was now a case of survival and Knox led his men back into their trenches, firing off a number of shots at the enemy using a rifle from a dead Rifleman. While he was withdrawing, Knox was hit in the left arm by a musket ball, and as he was having this wound bound up by a comrade they were both hit by a shower of grapeshot which killed his friend and caught Knox's smashed arm so that the shot remained embedded.

Knox was transported by mule ambulance to the medical post, a journey of agonising pain and torment as the cart trundled across the uneven ground, every vibration causing the shattered bones to grate. On his arrival at the station, the doctors wasted no time in administering chloroform, and amputated his arm completely from its socket. Despite the severity of his disablement and the crude surgery in the most insanitary conditions, John Knox was up and about seven days later and returned to his unit.

Knox had been noticed for his conspicuous gallantry at the battle of Alma, again at Inkerman, and now at Sebastopol with his latest display of great courage. He was awarded his Victoria Cross and later received the French

Legion d'Honneur, together with the Turkish Medal. He had the unique distinction of earning his VC as a Sergeant in the Scots Guards and as a Lieutenant in the Rifle Brigade. On 26 June 1857, he was present at the Review in Hyde Park when Queen Victoria pinned the coveted award on the tunics of the 62 recipients who paraded there. On this auspicious occasion Knox had the additional honour of being appointed Adjutant for the parade and carried out his duties with a presence that contributed to the success of this first presentation of a new award for gallantry.

The loss of his arm virtually put paid to his active service career. He had been appointed Acting Paymaster for the 2nd Battalion of the Rifle Brigade, and in January 1858 was transferred as Inspector of Musketry to the 4th Battalion. Promoted to Captain in April that year, he was in 1862 appointed Inspector of Musketry on Gibraltar. Returning to this country he held a similar post at Portsmouth in 1865.

In April 1872, Knox applied for and obtained the post of Prison Governor at Cardiff Gaol, following the dismissal of the previous Governor for serious offences relating to transport payments. There were eight candidates for the post, one of whom was already a prison governor, the others being Naval and Army officers. The appointment board of magistrates sat and voted on the merits of the applicants and after eliminating six names, it was a very close contest between John Knox and a local candidate Captain F.C. Knight of the Glamorgan Rifle Volunteers. After three votes John Knox was appointed. Despite his somewhat erratic education, he appears to have been a fairly prolific letter writer and was not averse to corresponding with those in high authority to further his claims. He also kept scrap books and notes of all events associated with his service. He had canvassed senior officers for his prison appointment and received useful references and some of his correspondence leaves no doubt that he saw himself as a man of courage.

While serving as a soldier he had appeared to be insensitive to the rigours of the battlefield and was often contemptuous of his fellows who struggled to cope with conditions. Strangely, in his role as prison governor, he was known as a man of kindness and understanding, and although he was a particularly strict disciplinarian, he was judged by both staff and prisoners to be fair and a patient listener to all grievances. He was said to be a model prison official and his arrival at Cardiff Gaol raised the morale of the staff and the establishment after years of mismanagement.

In September 1886 Knox was appointed to a larger prison at Kirkdale, Liverpool, thus coming within the scope of this book. He had received a Brevet Major rank from the Rifle Brigade when he went to Cardiff and now, with twelve years' prison service completed, he came to Liverpool with a distinguished reputation as a brave soldier and officer and as a fair-minded senior prison official. He had married Harriet Louisa Gale, daughter of R.C. Gale, of Winchester, and they had seven children. Their eldest child lived only three days and was born at Gibraltar; three were born at Southsea, including his only son, John Abercromby Knox (named after one of his father's colleagues in the Rifle Brigade who had been a Baronet) who died at Cardiff when only eleven years old; the fifth child, Edith May, was born in the Officer's Quarters at Chatham, and the two younger daughters were born at Cardiff. Three of the daughters, Harriet, Gladys and Winifred, were to marry clergymen. His wife suffered a severe stroke in January 1889 and died twelve months later in the Governor's House at Kirkdale Gaol. She is buried in Anfield Cemetery, Liverpool.

Major John Simpson Knox VC, in October 1891 following the closure of Kirkdale Prison, was appointed to the prison at Hull but ill-health precluded him from taking up the position and he was retired on pension from the prison service in April 1892. He left Liverpool to take up residence with his family at 6, Oriel Terrace, Cheltenham, where he died on 8 January 1897, almost 70 years old.

From humble beginnings in Glasgow and virtually by his very own efforts, Knox made a successful life in the service of his country, and in so doing earned the nation's highest award for bravery. His story did not end there, however. In 2000, a passing retired Brigadier noticed that the headstone on Knox's grave in Cheltenham was in a bad state of repair and in 2001, after much lobbying,

The grave of Major Knox VC

the headstone was refurbished by the Administrative Trustees of the Royal Green Jackets. His Victoria Cross is not publicly held.

(**Note** : Kirkdale Prison was on the site of what is now Kirkdale Recreation Ground and opposite the former site of Kirkdale Industrial School for Boys and Girls in Rumney Road.)

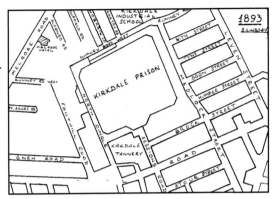

From the *Liverpool Courier*, 11 January 1897:

DEATH OF FORMER GOVERNOR OF KIRKDALE GAOL.

On, Friday, Major Knox V.C., a former Governor of Kirkdale Gaol, died at Cheltenham. The career of this prison governor was one of stirring incident, especially in his earlier days. His title showed that he had had a military career and that those who knew him and noticed that he had only one arm could appreciate the fact that he had not been a soldier without participating in the risks and sharing the privations of war. Major Knox entered the Army as a private in the Scots Fusilier Guards, and as a non-commissioned officer served in the Crimean War. It was one of the battles of that prolonged and what in the light of subsequent history may well be considered useless as well as costly struggle, that Major Knox was wounded and lost his arm.

He distinguished himself by his bravery, and was awarded that most coveted of all distinctions, the Victoria Cross, and also a commission. After he was invalided home he entered the Prison Service becoming Governor of several large establishments in succession including Kirkdale where he remained until it was closed. He then retired on a well merited pension to Cheltenham.

*A*ndrew Moynihan
VC

Andrew Moynihan VC

A ndrew Moynihan was born on 1 January 1830, at Saw Yard, Wakefield, Yorkshire, the youngest son of Malachi Moynihan and Ann (née Scott). (The *Register of the Victoria Cross* shows his date of birth as 8 September 1830.) His father, who was born in Ireland, gave his occupation as 'of the military profession' and is believed to have been the first Moynihan to settle in England, after the bulk of their money from their estates at Templemore in Tipperary, had dwindled away.

Malachi Moynihan, according to Plarr's *Lives of the Fellows, an account of the lives of Fellows of the Royal College of Surgeons* died in 1837 in Sefton Park, Liverpool when Andrew was six years old. His mother, however, lived for another 38 years after her husband's sad demise, dying in 1875, aged 87.

While Andrew was a young child, the family moved across the border to Dukinfield, in Lancashire, where they lived in Crescent Road. As a member of a large and now impoverished family, Andrew had few advantages of education, although he did attend the Wesleyan Methodist School, in Mill Lane, Ashton-under-Lyne and there learned reading, writing and arithmetic. On leaving school he worked for a short while in Mr. Wright's cotton mill (Flash Hill Mill in Old Street, Ashton), and from there moved to the mill of James Ogden & Sons, back in Dukinfield, where he was employed as a piecer. He was a good worker who was able to learn the skills very quickly, a talent which he later displayed during his military career.

Aged 17 years, he enlisted in the 90th Regiment, also known as the 'Perthshire Volunteers Light Infantry', then stationed in the barracks at Ashton. It was his earnest desire to follow the family tradition and become a soldier, and no doubt he was fully aware of their reputation, for it is claimed that in 1709 at the battle of Malplaquet, within the space of a few hours, five Moynihan brothers were killed on the battlefield. They liked to be in the thick of the fight. Andrew was keen and enthusiastic and took advantage of the chance to build up his physique through exercises and drill, and his learning ability on parade and in the art of musketry soon earned him promotion to the rank of Lance Corporal. Within two years he was posted to the barracks at Salford, to spend twelve months there as a drill instructor.

The regiment moved from Salford to Buttevant Barracks in County Cork, and on 18 February 1851 Moynihan was promoted Corporal. This part of the regiment was dispatched to the city of Cork to carry out the duty of guarding convicts on Spike Island, and after nearly twelve months during which he had also served as drill sergeant, they rejoined the regiment in Dublin. Here, on the 11 May 1853, he was promoted to full Sergeant and on the last day of that year he married Ellen Anne Parkin, the daughter of Thomas Parkin, a cabinet-maker from Hurst which is in the vicinity of both Ashton and Dukinfield, at Ashton Parish Church. Although her father made a steady living at his craft, he was in no position to accrue great wealth, and so the newly-weds were to start their married life in rather impecunious circumstances.

In 1854, preparations were being made for the 90th Regiment to embark for service in India on a normal tour of duty, and this would have taken place later in the year had not the Crimean campaign intervened. After the setbacks encountered there, the regiment's plans were changed and it was ordered to embark for the Russian war. Andrew Moynihan had been told to stay behind with the regimental depot, but in spite of his marital state he volunteered, to be replaced at the depot by a Sergeant Quinlan who was older and married with three young children.

Moynihan was determined to be in the action, and so with his regiment he set off from Kingstown aboard the steamship *Europa* bound for Sebastopol on 20 November 1854. (The *Europa* was a Cunarder of some 1800 tonnes built in 1848, used as a troop transporter in 1854 and then sold to become a sailing barque.) Within days of landing they found themselves in the trenches before the walls of the fortified side of the besieged port, a precursor of the trench warfare of the Great War, and were part of the 2nd Brigade commanded by Major General Buller. It was not the best time of the year to be in trenches for soon the Russian winter fell upon them and although there were many skirmishes between both sides there was no chance for a major engagement. The cold and the wet, together with a considerable amount of sickness, took a heavy toll of the British troops in their exposed positions. When spring came they were subjected to nightly harassment from Russian patrols, and Moynihan demonstrated his great courage and musketry skills in a number of these attacks, routing any enemy who came close to the British lines. On 18 June it was decided to assault the walls of the fortress but the regiment was held in reserve, much to Moynihan's disappointment. The attack was, however, a ghastly failure and cost the lives of many men as the defenders cut them down by firing from the walls.

The fortress structure was known as the Redan, being in the shape of a V, the apex of which faced the British troops, and on 8 September 1855 a second attempt to storm the fort was made; here the courage of Moynihan earned him the Victoria Cross. There were 300 men in a storming party together with 100 men in support, and they had been briefed by General Sir William Codrington on the importance of the action. Moynihan was one of the storming party and by all accounts was the first man into the Redan, even before the ladder parties had made it to the top, so that he was alone for a time facing the Russians. The good account he gave of himself served as a source of encouragement to his men. Firing as quickly as he could reload his gun, he shot a number of the enemy as they closed on him. The attackers were driven back, and Moynihan found himself alone except for a wounded officer, Lieutenant Arthur Swift, whom he attempted to rescue but who later died.

Completely outnumbered, he stood no chance. He was bayoneted twice and taken prisoner, but soon there was another attack by the British which took the Russians by surprise and in the course of events he was freed and immediately took up position with a number of others to take a toll of the enemy. It was short lived, for a violent Russian onslaught eventually drove them back to their trenches. Moynihan and Major Maude (Major Frederick Maude, later General, who earned his VC at the Redan on 5 September 1855) were among the last to withdraw. Both had been wounded, Maude rather seriously, and although weakened by his own wounds and exertions Moynihan carried the Major on his back out of the Redan. They were fired on as he stumbled across the open ground and once or twice he fell but rose to his feet and carried on until he was able to hand over the officer to those in the advance trench. He had barely regained his own regimental trench when he heard that Captain William Tinling was lying wounded, and although his own wounds were still bleeding and he was almost exhausted, Moynihan volunteered to go with Colour Sergeant Charles Saunderson and bring the badly wounded Captain back from the Redan trench.

Moynihan's award was gazetted on 24 February 1857, by which time he had received a commission as an Ensign on 2 May 1856, having previously held the rank of Sergeant Major. For such promotion to come through the ranks was extremely rare in those days. Usually it could only happen if the commission was purchased. Moynihan was in no position to do this but his performance as a soldier with tremendous leadership qualities impressed everyone with whom he came into contact. He was among the first men to receive the award from Queen Victoria in the memorable presentation of 26 June 1857 at Hyde Park, London, when she decorated 62 officers and men, including John Simpson Knox, (see elsewhere in this volume). Moynihan returned home to Dukinfield in 1856, where, in the Astley Arms, he was given a rapturous welcome and was presented with an inscribed watch. This would have been before his award was actually Gazetted.

In the Crimean campaign, Moynihan was Mentioned in Despatches, and won one each of the eleven Turkish and eight French medals that were awarded to his Regiment. On gaining his commission he was appointed to the 8th Regiment of Foot (later to become The King's Liverpool Regiment), and on 16 September 1857 was promoted to the rank of Lieutenant and sailed with his new regiment to India, to become involved in the suppression of the Indian Mutiny.

Once the regiment had become established it made its base in the area of Agra, and from here detachments were sent out on expeditions to the villages to fight the bands of mutineers who had infested them and the surrounding scrubland. One detachment left Agra on 11 March 1858, under the command of Captain George Corry, with Lieutenants Moynihan and Whelan, and 208 NCOs and privates forming part of a flying column, commanded by Brigadier St George Daniel Showers. The mutineers in considerable strength had occupied an entrenched village that was situated among the ravines of the Chimbul. The Kingsmen were split into two companies and, attacking in skirmishing order, drove the enemy out and pursued them for four miles, killing over a hundred of them in the process, without loss to the King's. Moynihan also took part in the capture of the towns of Bhujah and Seorale, particularly telling experiences for troops not long out from England against an enemy well-accustomed to the terrain and conditions, and often aided by the local inhabitants. He served throughout the Oudh campaign and played an important role in the capture of the fortress town of Sandee, so that for two years he was on truly active service in India.

A happy feature of his service here was that he had been able to bring his wife out with him. At the time of their embarkation she was expecting a child and it was a traumatic time for both of them as the previous year they had suffered the sad experience of losing male twins who were stillborn. To their great happiness a daughter was born, christened Ada Augusta, and the family stayed on until Andrew sailed for England from Calcutta in the *Monica* on 5 April 1860. The journey, though typical of the time, was fraught with tragedy, mainly from cholera, and the Moynihans justifiably feared for the survival of their two year old daughter but survive she did - in fact in 1881 she was shown in the Census as living in Withington as a governess, and was described as having been 'born at sea'.

On 25 September 1863, the 2nd Bn KLR embarked on board HMTransport *Orontes* (built by Lairds and launched in November 1862), bound for the Mediterranean, and on 1 October disembarked on the island of Malta where the troops occupied Verdala Barracks. Andrew Moynihan was promoted to the rank of Captain on 9 October and given command of 'the worst company in the Battalion' - they were known as the 'blackguards of No.5'. None of these men could read or write; they were slovenly and incompetent in their personal affairs which led to a great deal of unrest between them and other troops; they generally had a poor reputation. Moynihan was not dismayed by the prospects facing him, for in spite of his toughness as a soldier he was a kindly man with great patience and understanding. He tackled the problem of illiteracy with vigour and taught his men to read and write sufficiently well for them to write home. This gave them some self-respect which in turn changed their attitude towards their general appearance and behaviour. It was not easy, but it was worthwhile, and he claimed that this achievement gave him as much satisfaction as did his victories at war.

It was custom on the island to drink goat's milk, cow's milk being scarce, and it appears that there was an infection carried in the milk of the goat that at the time was not understood - but resulted in Malta Fever (Brucellosis). In May 1867, Andrew Moynihan was struck down having drunk fresh goat's milk and died on 19 May 1867, aged 37 years. He was buried in Ta Braxia Cemetery, Malta, with a full military funeral attended by all the officers of both battalions of The King's Regiment, and by Major General M.K. Atherley, of Malta Command.

Andrew and Ellen Moynihan had had two more children. Eva Ellen was born in Ireland in 1862 and baptized at Templemore, the former ancestral home of the Moynihans. Their happiness appeared complete when on 2 October 1865, in Malta, a son, Berkeley George Andrew Moynihan, was born. Tragically, Andrew, who had brought great honour to the family with his Victoria Cross and the success he achieved during his Army career was never to know the great success his son was to achieve.

In 1871, Ellen Moynihan was living with her married sister Mary, who was married to Alfred Ball, a police inspector, and Ellen's children, Eva and Berkley, at Mary's home at 5 Woodhouse Square, Leeds. Ellen was in receipt of a pension of £1 per week from the Army.

* * *

Berkley Moynihan was educated in Leeds and then at the Bluecoat School and in 1883, at the age of eighteen, declared that he would not follow the Moynihan tradition and join the Army. Instead he declared to his very relieved mother that he wanted to save lives rather than kill, and so in the autumn of that year he entered medical school. Life for Mrs. Moynihan had not been easy at any time; money was always scarce and yet she had managed to uphold the standards that she had valued so much. Berkeley knew only too well the sacrifices she must have made to keep the family going and he worked remorselessly to make the grade. He had inherited his father's ability to learn quickly and his conscientious efforts paid off in 1887 when he graduated from London University with the degree of Bachelor of Medicine. In April 1890, he was appointed Residential Surgical officer at the Leeds Infirmary, and this was to be an important association. He rose from near poverty to become one of the richest medical men in the country and was knighted in 1912. Plarr's *Lives of the Fellows* points out that money was not his motivation, as is evidenced by his readiness to treat the poorer patients free of charge.

In 1908 he was commissioned into the Royal Army Medical Corps (Territorial), and on 28 November 1914 was promoted to Temporary Colonel, Army Medical Service and served in France. In 1919, he was demobilised with the rank of Major General. From 1916 to 1919 he was Chairman of the Council of Consultants and also of the Army Advisory Board, and in 1929 was created Baron Moynihan of Leeds. He was world famous as a brilliant surgeon, a master of his craft, a man with a most remarkable life story who had a quite remarkable father. In 1895 he married Isabella Wellesley Jessop who died in Leeds on 31 August 1936. Berkley Moynihan died six days later. Lord (Colin) Moynihan, presently Chairman of the British Olympic Association, is the great-great-grandson of Andrew Moynihan VC. It is said that Lord (Berkley) Moynihan, on every anniversary of his father's winning his Victoria Cross, always dined at home with his family at a table decorated by his daughter, Dorothy, with red roses in the form of a Victoria Cross. After dinner he would take out his father's sword and VC and talk about his parents' lives.

In 1996, a blue plaque was unveiled at the Astley Arms to commemorate the reception Andrew Moynihan VC had received there in 1856. In 2005, to celebrate the 150th anniversary of Moynihan's earning his Victoria Cross, Lord Colin Moynihan unveiled a gold plaque above the blue plaque. The *Manchester Evening News* then ran a story relating how Andrew's name had been misspelt on the gold plaque, being shown as Moyniham, and speculated as to whether Lord Moynihan had noticed it.

John O'Neill
VC MM

John O'Neill was born on 27 January 1897 at 13, Forsyth Street, Airdrie, Lanark, Scotland, the third of four sons and one daughter of Irish-born Samuel O'Neill and Agnes (née Devan). His father worked as a coal miner in one of the local collieries. In 1901, Samuel and Agnes, with their five children were living in New Monkland, Lanarkshire. It is believed that, on leaving school, John joined his father in the pits. However, there is a suggestion that Samuel O'Neill, before 1914, came down to Liverpool where he joined Liverpool City Police – unfortunately Merseyside Police have been unable to confirm this. John's mother died in 1901, possibly in childbirth as her daughter was born that same year.

John O'Neill VC MM

With the outbreak of war in August 1914, O'Neill enlisted in the 2nd Battalion of the Prince of Wales's Leinster Regiment, (Royal Canadians), and on 13 April 1915 was posted to France. While in France he had the reputation of being almost fearless, and was awarded the Military Medal for 'bravery in the field'. He was promoted to Sergeant and was quite happy to be at the front of the fight and to lead by example.

During the great British advance in October 1918, O'Neill earned the nation's highest award for gallantry. At this stage of the war, trench warfare was being replaced by field warfare, largely as a result of the use of tanks to support an infantry advance. Although the Germans were withdrawing they were not running away but were contesting every yard of ground. As the Leinsters struck out from the front at Ypres towards the bitterly contested ground around the fortified town of Courtrai, progress was slow but they moved steadfastly forward to the north-west and were between Ledeghem and Moorseele, some six miles from Courtrai, when their advance was checked by heavy fire from two machine-guns and an artillery battery firing over open sights. Sergeant O'Neill, leading only eleven men, charged the field battery, taking the four field guns, two machine-guns, and sixteen prisoners. Six days later, on 20 October, with only one man to cover him, he rushed an enemy machine-gun position, routing about 100 of the enemy and causing many casualties. It was stated in his citation that 'throughout the operations he displayed the most remarkable courage and powers of leadership'.

The intensity of the fighting, and the strong, bitter resistance encountered by the Leinsters, is evidenced by the fact that during October they advanced some 10,000 yards and took five villages, capturing more than 300 prisoners, together with 66 machine-guns and twelve field guns. A second Victoria Cross was awarded to Private Martin Moffatt, a member of the 2nd Battalion of the Leinsters, on the very same day as O'Neill and at the same location but in a separate incident. It has been said that at the time O'Neill earned his VC he had been told by a man in the 36th Ulster Division that O'Neill's younger brother had been killed and that John O'Neill went forward in a mood of revenge. It transpired that his brother had not been killed but had been wounded.

On 2 August 1919, the King held an Investiture in the Quadrangle of Buckingham Palace and decorated Sergeant John O'Neill with the Victoria Cross. It was a rather unusual occasion for, after the servicemen attending had been honoured, the King presented the Victoria Cross to the widow of Major Charles Yate of the King's Own Yorkshire Light Infantry who won his VC on 26 August 1914 at Le Cateau, but whose death shortly afterwards was not revealed by the Germans until after the war. The King also presented the Albert Medal to the widow of Private Arthur Johnson. The Investiture was attended by the Prince of Wales, as Colonel-in-Chief of the Leinster Regiment and by Field Marshal The Duke of Connaught, music being supplied by the Band of the Coldstream Guards. In the afternoon the King received representatives of the Indian Army who were in London for the peace celebrations under the command of Brigadier E.W. Costello VC.

On the following day John O'Neill was granted the Freedom of the Burgh of Hamilton and received a gift of £400. Apart from the VC, MM, and his war service medals, he also held the French *Medaille Militaire* and a Belgian decoration, Knight of the Order of Leopold.

On 6 February 1920, as Colonel-in-Chief of the 2nd Battalion Leinster Regiment, the Prince of Wales motored to Colchester to present honours and medals to officers and men of the regiment. His Royal Highness was met outside the town by Sergeant O'Neill V.C., who travelled with him to the barrack square, where 100 men received decorations. In a brief address the Prince said he was very proud that the King had made him Colonel-in-Chief of the regiment, which had a very splendid war record, taking part in all the major engagements and alas, suffering very heavy casualties. He sympathised with the comrades of the fallen, and alluded to the glorious traditions of the regiment which had been fully maintained by the battalion. In conclusion he urged all the young soldiers on parade to 'Follow and live up to the splendid example set by the men who fought and won in the Great War'.

The Leinster Regiment was disbanded in 1922 as part of the post-war plan for the Army, and O'Neill tried to adjust by going back to the coal mines, but on 25 April 1923 he enlisted in the Royal Air Force. While in the RAF he became quite friendly with T.E. Lawrence (Lawrence of Arabia), who had assumed the name of J.H. Ross, changing this again to T.E. Shaw, and was introduced to many of Lawrence's friends including members of the Royal Family. O'Neill rose once more to the rank of sergeant having learned the trade of Armourer, and had completed 16 years service when he was discharged on 27 July 1939. He had spent much of his service with the RAF Marine Branch and had served aboard the aircraft carrier H.M.S. *Glorious*. Less than 12 months later *Glorious*, with her escort destroyers *Acasta* and *Ardent*, was intercepted in the Norwegian Sea by the German battleships *Gneisenau* and *Scharnhost*. All three ships were sunk within two hours, with the loss of over 1500 officers and men of the Royal Navy, Royal Marines and the Royal Air Force. Only 39 survivors were picked up.

With war declared only six weeks after his discharge it was not long before O'Neill was back in uniform, this time with a commission in the Pioneer Corps with 295 Company, part of 17 Group Army Pioneer Corps, based at Huyton near Liverpool. He served with the military escort aboard the troopship *Dunera* when she was engaged in transporting over 2,000 deportees from Liverpool to Australia, including Jews of German origin. (The film *The Dunera Boys* starring Bob Hoskins deals with this episode). Back on Merseyside, the unit, which was largely concerned with protecting the docks and cargoes, was billeted in Hoylake and West Kirby. They gave valuable service during the heavy air raids in the dock area.

Lieutenant John O'Neill VC, MM died on 16 October 1942 of a heart attack, aged 45 years. He was given a full military funeral and is buried in Holy Trinity churchyard, Hoylake. On 18 February 1922 he had married Kathleen O'Neill Flanagan, who had been employed as a dressmaker in Hamilton, and they set up home there at 19, Moore Street, Cadzow. They had two daughters.

On 13 February 1962 O'Neill's medal group, including his VC, was placed with Messrs B.A. Seaby, coin dealers, in Great Portland Street, London for sale by auction. That same day, thieves broke into the premises via a car showroom situated beneath their offices and burned open three safes, stealing coins and medals valued then at £30,000. Amongst the medals were those of General Thomas Brisbane, after whom the capital of Queensland, Australia, was named, and those of John O'Neill. Despite a substantial reward of £2,000 being offered, nothing was ever again heard of any of the stolen medals.

The grave of John O'Neill at Hoylake

In 2004, cadets from the Air Training Corps, while cleaning the cemetery at Hoylake, discovered John O'Neill's grave. Members of the newly formed Leinster Regiment Association had the headstone and grave cleaned and reconsecrated, placing a plaque on the grave indicating that O'Neill earned his VC whilst serving with that Regiment. A service was held at St Hildeburgh's Church, Hoylake, attended by members of his family from Sussex and Lanarkshire and by Major General David O'Morchol, President of the Royal Leinster Association, who travelled from County Wexford and proudly announced that his father and his two uncles had all served with John O'Neill in the Great War with the Leinster Regiment. On 11 November 2005 Mr. Vincent McGough, Chairman of the Association, laid a wreath on the grave.

Edward Unwin
VC CB CMG

Edward Unwin VC CB CMG

E dward Unwin was born on 16 March 1864 at Forest Lodge, Fawley, Hythe, Hampshire, the son of Edward Wilberforce Unwin JP, and Henrietta Jane, daughter of Captain and Mrs. Carmac. In the 1871 Census Edward is listed as the third eldest of seven children, although it appears from the records that Edward, his father, was married twice. The first wife, Penelope (née Ellis) whom he married in 1849, died in 1854 and was almost certainly the mother of his two older daughters, one of whom, Penelope Lesley, was born in the year her mother died. His father married Henrietta Jane Carmac in 1856, and she was the mother of Edward Junior and his younger siblings. Edward Senior died in 1888 while Henrietta lived until 1902.

Edward Junior was first educated at Miss Hill's School in Cheltenham, and then at Mr. Charles Gedge's School in Malvern Wells. Charles Gedge was the son of an agricultural labourer and did well to end up as a 'National schoolmaster' who in the 1891 Census is shown as 'retired elementary schoolmaster with Government'.

On leaving school, Edward joined the training ship HMS *Conway*, stationed in the River Mersey. He left *Conway* in 1880, his strong character in no way subdued following two dozen strokes of the birch he had once received on board for some youthful misdemeanour. He went off to sea as an apprentice on the fast mail ship *Roslyn Castle*, one of Donald Currie's Castle Line vessels, and later sailed with the P & 0 Line. He had a short spell in the Egyptian Navy before enlisting in the Royal Navy on 16 October 1895. At that time the Navy was short of watch-keeping and navigation officers and Edward was transferred and commissioned as a Lieutenant. He served in the punitive Benin River Expedition of 1897 and was in the Fleet manoeuvres of 1899, serving on the guard ship *Thunderer*. He later served in South Africa in 1900, was promoted Lieutenant Commander in October 1903, and retired from the Navy in 1909 with the rank of Commander.

On 29 July 1914 he was recalled on mobilisation and appointed Fleet Coaling Officer to Admiral Lord Jellico on HMS *Iron Duke*, the first British battleship fitted with anti-aircraft guns in 1914. Named after Wellington, she was the flagship of the Grand Fleet. Unwin had amassed special knowledge in the construction and design of colliers and had practical experience in the handling of coaling barges and lighters. It was as a result of this experience that he became a prime mover in using a collier, with barges, as an assault ship at Gallipoli. Although there was some opposition to the plan, Admiral Wemyss (whose first name coincidentally was 'Rosslyn') authorised the use of the 4000 ton collier *River Clyde* as transport and lighters would be used to act as a floating bridge to enable the troops to get ashore.

In theory, the plan was to attack V beach on the tip of Cape Helles, on the Gallipoli peninsula. The battleship HMS *Albion* and other warships were to bombard the Turkish positions and flatten the barbed wire defences erected on the beaches. When the great invasion fleet for Gallipoli gathered at Mudros, a fine natural harbour used as the British Naval Base on the island of Lemnos, Unwin was in command of HMS *Hussar*, an old torpedo gunboat built in 1894 which had been used as a communications centre for the Commander-in-Chief and converted into a minesweeper. This was in February and March of 1915 and Unwin, now a man of 50 years of age, could not have foreseen that in a matter of a few weeks he would earn the country's highest award for bravery.

He was given command of the *River Clyde*, with the acting rank of Captain. What followed was a nightmare. At 6.00 am on Sunday 25 April 1915, the *Albion* and other warships closed in and bombarded enemy positions almost ceaselessly for about an hour, before the *River Clyde*, now laden with infantry and artillery, together with her barges moved into her disembarking position. The barges, after a few hitches, were duly deployed to form a floating bridge across which the troops spewed forth - to be met with the most withering machine gun fire imaginable. The *River Clyde's* gangways were strewn with dead and wounded; only a few men reached shore and they were in dire straits and unable to move on. It was estimated afterwards that the enemy unleashed some 10,000 rounds per minute at the height of the fray. It was not possible to get the main force ashore until darkness fell that night, and that anybody got ashore at all was almost entirely due to the gallantry and physical stamina of the officers and men of the *River Clyde*. They were really magnificent in their endeavours to make the operation succeed in spite of the terrible setbacks.

Edward Unwin was a large, bluff, cheery man, with broad shoulders and a blunt manner, and he was not afraid to 'muck in' when things were rough. When evening came on that frightful day and preparations were being made for further landings, another problem arose. His plan had been to beach his ship and use hoppers or lighters to form a bridge to shore but they were unable to secure the bridge to the beach because of enemy activity and the current swept the barges apart. Unwin himself swam ashore with a line, and secured the first lighter, towing it to the shore, but as there was no means of fastening the line he stood in the water with the line round his waist, like a human bollard, taking the strain as the first parties of troops rushed over him. Four other members of his crew (Midshipmen Drewry and Malleson, Able Seaman William Williams and Seaman George Samson) joined him in trying to keep the barges together, and as they struggled so the enemy swept the area with machine gun fire. They each made numerous attempts to secure the lighters and Williams was killed. The cold and the immersion began to tell on Unwin after a while, and he was forced to return to his ship where the doctor wrapped him in blankets, but as soon as his circulation returned he ignored the doctor's advice and went back to the barges; he was wounded three times. As morning came he decided he must try to recover some of the wounded men lying in the shallow water by the beach. He commandeered a launch, secured her stern to the *River Clyde* and then punted her to the shore, rescued seven or eight men by man-handling them into his boat, and took them back to the old collier. In the end he was forced by sheer exhaustion to stop and rest.

The assault failed because following the naval bombardment in the morning and before our troops had landed, three platoons of Turkish infantry with machine guns returned to find that their trenches and the barbed wire had hardly been damaged by the naval shells, and so were able to cut down the assault troops with very little difficulty. In addition to Unwin, Drewry, Malleson, Williams and Samson also received the Victoria Cross. Both Williams and Samson had previously served with Unwin aboard HMS *Hussar*.

As a result of his wounds, Unwin went home for an operation in Haslar Hospital, Alverstoke, Hampshire, but was back in the port of Mudros, on 1 July 1915, in command of the cruiser *Endymion*, one of the Edgar Class which were considered to be unsuitable for their designated role in the blockade of Germany and were replaced in 1915, then sent to serve in the Dardanelles. Unwin was beach-master for the landings at Suvla Bay on 7 August and again for the evacuations in December. He was the last to leave the beaches and as he was leaving he saw a man fall overboard; Unwin jumped into the sea and rescued him. General Julian Byng, who witnessed the rescue, is reported to have told Commodore Roger Keyes: 'You really must do something about Unwin! You should send him home – we want several little Unwins!'

In January 1916, he attended an investiture to receive his Victoria Cross from King George V, at Buckingham Palace. In March 1916 he was admitted to the Order of St Michael and St George (CMG) and was in command of the light cruiser *Amethyst* on the South-East America station from March until October 1916. In January 1917 he was appointed Principal Naval Transport Officer in Egypt (receiving the Order of the Nile). In the early part of 1918, he was the Principal Naval Transport Officer for the Eastern Mediterranean, being promoted Commodore in 1919 and retiring in 1920 with the rank of Captain.

On 24 April, 1897 he married Evelyn Agnes Carey, the daughter of Major General William Dobree Carey, of Guernsey, and they had two sons and two daughters. They moved to Ashbourne, Derbyshire on his retirement, and then went to live at Hindhead, in Surrey, where he died on 19 April 1950; he is buried in nearby Grayshott. Evelyn Agnes, his wife, died in 1948. His Victoria Cross is on permanent loan to the Imperial War Museum. Between 1905 and 1912 he lived at 12 Helena Road, Southsea, and this house is marked by a Blue Plaque. Interestingly, his ancestor, James Unwin, was a friend of Thomas Gainsborough, the celebrated English portrait painter, who painted James's wife, Frances. Her portrait remained within the family until 1928, when Edwin Unwin VC sold it for Canadian $74,671.

In the *Liverpool Courier* of Tuesday 29 July 1919 there was an item headed:

Old Conway Boy's V.C.' - Presentation to Liverpool Commander ...

An interesting little ceremony took place at the Town Hall yesterday, when the Lord Mayor, Lieut. Colonel Ritchie, at the request of the Imperial Merchant Service Guild, presented a war medallion to an old CONWAY cadet, Commodore Edward Unwin V.C., C.M.G., R.N.

The occasion drew a large company of ladies and gentlemen connected with various organisations having close relations with the sea. As explained by Lieut. T.W. Moore, R.N.R., the secretary of the Guild, the medallion was struck by a Liverpool ship owner for presentation to those of the crew of the steamer RIVER CLYDE who were awarded the Victoria Cross for services rendered at the landing at Gallipoli. He read the official account of Admiral Roebeck of that memorable exploit, in which high praise was bestowed on Commodore Unwin, who was in command of the vessel, and who it was stated, at one critical period of the operations was standing up to his waist in water under very heavy fire directing the work.

The Lord Mayor in making the presentation, said it afforded him the very greatest pleasure as Chief Magistrate, to have the honour of handing the medallion to one who had so richly deserved everything that had been said of his services. Whatever might be the criticisms as to the operations at Gallipoli, there could only be one opinion as to the gallantry and devotion of those who took part in the landing.

Commodore Unwin said he could not say with what pleasure he received that medallion, nor could he say that he deserved it; but he could say that he saw something of what went on at that beach, and he would like them all to realise not what he did, but what the Army did. The men who landed there were, one and all, VCs much more than he was. An enormous number of VCs were won on that beach that had never been heard of.

On the motion of Captain Jackman, chairman of the Imperial Merchant Service Guild, and seconded by Captain Whitehead, president of the Mercantile Marine Service Association, a cordial vote of thanks was passed to the Lord Mayor.

In acknowledging the vote, his Lordship commented on the unity which the war had been the means of bringing about between the Navy and the Mercantile Marine, and said it is a matter in which all in Liverpool closely connected with the sea as it was, would rejoice.

Similar sentiments had been expressed in the *Journal of Commerce* dated 2 December 1916, when the Lord Mayor of Liverpool (Mr. Max Muspratt) presented a Sword of Honour to Sub-Lieutenant George Leslie Drewry VC, RNR, attended by other officers who served with him and Unwin in the

Dardanelles. The presentation was made on behalf of the Merchant Service Guild. The Lord Mayor added: 'Although we cannot as Liverpudlians claim Lieutenant Drewry as a Liverpool man, we can claim that Liverpool stands at the head of all ports in this Empire in connection with the mercantile marine, and it is right and proper that the greatest honour should be paid in Liverpool to Lieutenant Drewry, who is the first member of the mercantile marine to gain the Victoria Cross'. Sadly, George Drewry VC was to lose his life at Scapa Flow on 3 August 1918.

(There is an interesting coincidence regarding Edward Unwin's retirement to the little hamlet of Hindhead in Surrey. On the War Memorial in St. Alban's Church in the village is the name of another *Conway* VC, Lieutenant Colonel Philip Eric Bent, of the 9th Battalion The Leicestershire Regiment. His mother came to England from Nova Scotia, bringing her son with her. They too settled in Derbyshire, at Ashby-de-la-Zouch, and later she moved south to Hindhead. Philip E. Bent died in action on 1 October 1917. [See page 7 in this volume].)

ADDENDA

Following the publication of Books 1 and 2 in this series, several readers have contacted me with additional information. I am most grateful to them, and would welcome any further contributions to add to our knowledge of 'Liverpool Heroes'.

Bill Sergeant

BOOK 1
Noel Godfrey CHAVASSE VC & Bar MC

Some nice little stories about Noel Chavasse have been brought to my notice and no doubt there will be more to follow! Steve Pritchard, who sells our books in his shop in Moor Lane, Crosby, tells how his grandfather, serving with the Liverpool Scottish in France, accidentally cut his finger rather badly on a tin of bully beef and sought treatment from the Medical Officer (Chavasse). 'The Doc' quickly dressed the wound whilst muttering under his breath about how he would be better employed looking after wounded volunteers than playing nurse to conscripted men. Later that day, Chavasse sought out Steve's grandfather, apologised to him, explaining that he now knew that he too was a volunteer and invited him to allow him to redress the wound – 'properly this time' - an insight into Chavasse's 'normalness'!

A Mr Roberts (sadly I have no further details) spoke to me in Liverpool Cathedral in August 2007 when we held a short service on the 90th Anniversary of Chavasse's death. Handing me a generous donation, he explained that his grandfather had been badly wounded in France and medical staff wanted to amputate his leg. Fortunately, Captain Chavasse, after examining the wound, decided to operate himself and managed to save the leg.

Mr Chris Mercier, now 91 years of age and himself a former pupil of Liverpool College, wrote to tell me that his late wife's father, Captain John Robert Dickinson MC & Bar, attended the College at about the same time as Noel Chavasse. He added that Edward Frederick Russell, 2nd Baron Russell of Liverpool, at the College at the same time, won a Military Cross and *two* bars in the Great War. He later became Deputy Judge Advocate General to the British Army on the Rhine and was one of the chief legal advisers during the Nazi war crime trials after the Second World War, and was the author of *Scourge of the Swastika*.

Mr John Robertson, Past President of Liverpool St Helens Rugby Club, accompanied a donation from the club with a note that both Noel and Christopher Chavasse played for the Club alongside Fred H. Turner, who was the Club Captain and also captain of Scotland in the season 1913-14. Turner enlisted on the outbreak of war and was killed in action – Noel Chavasse recovered and buried the body of his friend.

In November 2007, the Dingle Community Theatre performed at the Anglican Cathedral a play entitled *Noel Godfrey Chavasse VC & Bar*, specially written by local man Alan Bower. The play gave a poignant, entertaining and highly informative dramatic presentation of the life, deeds and death of Chavasse.

William CONNOLLY VC

There is still some uncertainty about William Connolly's marital status. In Book 1 I referred to a marriage in 1839 and suggested that this might be our William Connolly. Certainly in 1851 William Connolly, born 1817 in Liverpool, with his wife, Mary, born 1821 in Whitehaven, and their daughter Mary born 1848 in Liverpool, were living at 10 Upper Pitt Street, Liverpool. William, however, is described as a gilder and painter. In the 1861 Census, we find a William Connolly, born about 1821, unmarried, a 'pensioner of HEI Company', lodging at 124 Upper Mann Street, Liverpool, with a couple named Burrows. It is almost certain that 'HEI Company' refers to the Honourable East India Company, which would fit in with Connolly's service in India. In 1881, we find a William Connolly, Army Pensioner aged 60 years lodging with the Dodd family (not Dove as in Book 1) but he is now described as a *widower*. Maurice Rigby, who assisted Sid Lindsay with his research, suggests that William may have married between 1861 and 1866, his wife's name being Elizabeth. He points to a Census entry for 1871 in respect of William Connolly and Elizabeth living at 18 Mansfield Street, off St Ann Street, Liverpool and believes he found a record of a baptism in St Peter's, Liverpool, on 7 May 1866, of Henry, son of William and Elizabeth. The truth is that at present we just do not know! Maurice also refers to a baptism on 19 March 1822, possibly at St Peter's, of a William Connolly, son of Joseph and Hannah Connolly of School Lane, Liverpool. Again, this may be our man but we cannot be sure.

Hugh McDonald McKENZIE VC DCM

By mistake a photograph of William Ratcliffe VC MM was published instead of that of McKenzie – apologies! This is the correct photograph.

William RATCLIFFE VC MM

In recent weeks I have come across a wonderful photograph, held by Warrington Museum, of William Ratcliffe with three other VC winners from the South Lancashire Regiment: John Thomas Davies VC, Gabriel George Coury VC and

John Readitt VC. This was obviously a special occasion and a posed photograph. If anybody can help with a date and occasion, I would be very interested and grateful. Ratcliffe and Coury feature in Book 1, and Davies' story is in this book.

On 25 September 2007 Mrs Noreen Hill, great-niece of Ratcliffe, placed his medals, including his VC and MM, on loan with the Imperial War Museum, London, where they will shortly be on display. In Book 1 I also wrote about a plaque, commissioned by his fellow dockers and said to have hung in the Trade Union Office in South Liverpool but which was apparently lost when the offices were demolished. I am delighted to announce that the plaque has been found! Made of marble, it is in excellent condition. It has been in the possession of Mr Michael Kettle for a number of years, his grandfather having told Michael's father to make sure the plaque was saved. Michael's grandfather, like Ratcliffe, attended St Vincent's School, Park Lane, and the plaque, suitably cleaned but awaiting the photograph which was displayed with it, is to be placed in St Vincent's School as a constant reminder for future generations of the courage of one of its former pupils.

Left to right: John Readitt VC, Gabriel George Coury VC, John Thomas Davies VC and William Ratcliffe VC

BOOK 2
Edward Felix BAXTER VC

At the History Exhibition at St George's Hall, Liverpool in August 2007, Jan Hooker from Wallasey stopped to speak to us and subsequently sent me some press cuttings about Baxter which appeared under the caption 'Motor Cycling' on 3 October 1916, possibly in a magazine of the same name, describing him as the first motor cyclist to earn a Victoria Cross. Interestingly, in the article there is a photograph of and reference to another *'famous motor cyclist, Lieutenant O.C. Godfrey, who left for France some two or three weeks ago after recovering from a flying accident (and) is now reported missing. We are able to announce that he was last seen planing down with his machine under control into the German lines, evidently having suffered from engine trouble or the like. Lieutenant Godfrey has been in the thick of the fighting on the Somme since he arrived at the Front'.* Commonwealth War Graves Commission records show that Lieutenant Oliver Cyril Godfrey, Royal Flying Corps, of Finchley, London, was killed on 23 September 1916.

On 10 October 1916, the magazine reported that *'According to the Liverpool Press it is expected that some kind of public recognition will shortly be given to the heroism of the late Second Lieutenant Baxter VC. It has not yet been decided as to what form the memorial will take'.* Jan also sent me copies of some postcards, including one addressed to Mrs Baxter (Edwards's mother) in Kidderminster, apparently franked on 5 February 1916, reporting that *'Cake and Sweets arrived in good condition, also magazine...we are in trenches but having a more peaceable time this journey, Good news rolling in nowadays – we shall be home for Xmas!!'* Another card, addressed to his father and signed 'F' (Felix?), is French and depicts war damage. The name of the French village portrayed has been censored, but 'F' describes this as *'a specimen of the destruction seen in France. Am keeping in O.K. health and we are enjoying quite mild weather'.* How sad that within a few weeks of these cards, Baxter should lose his life.

Two other postcards, addressed to Mrs E.F. Baxter (his wife) but sent by 'B.A.B.' from Kidderminster (presumably his mother, Beatrice Anita) are dated September and November 1916, ie after his death, and show that Baxter's widow lived or stayed at that time at 105 Kingsley Road and 32 Falkner Square, Liverpool. One of the two postcards which seem to have come from Baxter VC shows a censored picture of *'the town where I tried to find Douglas but there were none of his crowd within five miles of it'.* The town is recognisable as Albert – but who was Douglas?

Richard George MASTERS VC

Through further conversations with (Richard) George Masters's nephew, John Masters, a mere youngster of 87 years, I identified several mistakes in his story in Book 2. George's mother was Margaret Harris Vittle Dony, who died in 1928. The

lady who renamed the RAF Vessel 5012 as RCT Vessel *Richard George Masters* was George's married daughter, Bessie, and not his sister, Bessie. The 100-yards sprint reportedly won by George Masters in 1916 was in fact won by his brother, John, the father of John Masters. In this context, John Masters showed me a cutting from the *Southport Visitor* in 1971 which told how John Masters Senior (George's brother), having been presented with an inscribed bracelet in 1916 when he won the 100-yards sprint in France with the 38th Welsh Division of the British Expeditionary Force, was unable to wear it in case it revealed their position by reflecting the sunlight. Consequently he carried the bracelet in his tunic pocket for the rest of the war. On his return to England he was unable to find the bracelet and presumed he had lost it in France but 53 years later, in 1971, the bracelet was found on the street in Southport and eventually returned to him. It is likely that he mislaid it upon his return to Southport in 1918. John Jnr has also given me a photograph (below), which shows his father, his Uncle George (VC) and their cycling trainer, Harry Hughes, whose sister, Sarah, married John Masters Snr. In front of them, with a smaller version of the bicycles the two men are holding, is a young boy aged about 5 years. John

Masters Jnr explains that the photograph was taken in about 1925 and the young boy is himself! The cut-down bicycle he had was specially made for him by his Uncle George. John remembers that Uncle George used to visit his brother and their family every Tuesday afternoon, when he and John's father would sit talking about dogs and cycling, but never about the war. George Masters' younger brother, David William, served in the North Lancashire Regiment and was killed in action in France on 10 March 1918. John

Masters Snr served in the Royal Army Service Corps in the Great War, while John Jnr served in the RAF in the Second World War. Because David William was regularly referred to as William, Richard George Masters did not have a brother called William, but his youngest brother, born in 1892, was John Masters Senior.

John also supplied me with a rather imposing photograph of his Uncle George proudly wearing his medals.

George Edward NURSE VC

Jack Hawksett from Wirral contacted me to describe how, as a young teenager, he used to deliver the old accumulator batteries in the Durning Road area of Liverpool and regularly delivered to the home of George Nurse in Crosfield Road. He says George was a smartly dressed, quietly spoken, respectful gentleman who often called into the shop which supplied the accumulators to talk about the progress of the Second World War with the proprietor, Mr Evans, another old soldier. He believes that George suffered for many years with chest problems and describes how he always wore a muffler and coat, even when in his own home. He concludes by stating that George was a 'very generous man and gave me a shilling for Christmas'!

Arthur Herbert PROCTER VC

Mrs Maureen Lenton, niece of Arthur Herbert Procter, contacted me from York to say that Arthur had a third brother, her father Cecil Frederick Procter, born in 1903, who came to live in Liverpool, joined the Mersey Pilot Service and then lived the rest of his life in Boxdale Road, Liverpool 18. He was one of the pilots at the launch of the Cammell Laird-built 4th *Ark Royal* in 1950. She also informed me that her cousin, Cecil, son of Arthur Herbert, was killed in the Second World War. He was Sergeant Cecil Charles Procter, 86 Squadron, Royal Air Force, who died aged 20 years on 21 July 1941, when his father was Chaplain, and is commemorated on the RAF Memorial at Runnymede. Arthur Herbert Procter is also commemorated by the naming of a road in Birkenhead. Arthur and his wife had a 4th son who died in infancy.

APPENDIX I

Sid Lindsay's Introduction to Book I, and his notes on the Victoria Cross

(Sid Lindsay was a local Victoria Cross enthusiast and historian, whose work on local Victoria Cross heroes has inspired the production of this series of books. Sadly, Sid passed away without knowing that his findings, augmented by later research, were to be published, but he would have been delighted to know that his 'Heroes' were to be remembered in this way. **Bill Sergeant**)

This collection of notes came about as a result of some private research I did into the businesses and trades of Merseyside. Whilst thus engaged, in 1986 I came across the name of Captain Gabriel George Coury VC, who with his family was involved in the Liverpool Cotton Trade. It then occurred to me that there was no record of local recipients of the Victoria Cross in one collection, and I decided to attempt to rectify this omission. I naively believed that the lives of such heroes would be well-documented and that all I would need to do was to draw up a list of names and quickly gather together the stories of their deeds and lives.

Sid Lindsay at George Nurse VC's grave, Allerton, Liverpool

I began with an initial list of 20 names but this number soon rose to 62, some admittedly having only a slight connection with Merseyside. I had not anticipated that for many of these heroes there was little on record other than birth, death and citation. To my disappointment I quickly found that the most likely sources, such as Regimental Associations and Museums and the Royal British Legion were not the best informed and in some instances, sadly, seemed to be uninterested. As a mere novice in such matters, this lack of response caused me considerable frustration and meant that the project took much longer than I had anticipated.

I am not a military historian, nor am I a proficient storyteller. Consequently, this is simply meant to be a collection of biographical notes about some very special people. Inevitably, there will be mistakes due to my lack of expertise. I have made many errors while researching, but each has served only to make me seek another direction to find out what I needed to know. Compared to the depth of research which goes into the writing of some of the major tomes to which I have had access, my task has been of a comparatively short duration. Nevertheless it has tested my patience, as well as that of my longsuffering wife, Betty, to the limits. It has made me realise, above all, how important it is that similar exercises are undertaken to ensure that other aspects of our local history are recorded for posterity. I urge anybody who can do so to make their contribution by jotting down notes on their own lives, their family history, the firm for which they work or worked, military and public service or just memories of things that used to be. Otherwise, as with my gallant subjects, this information will be lost. Believe me, the satisfaction to be gained is considerable.

My enquiries have brought me into contact with many correspondents who share my interest in the lives of these heroic figures, awarded the nation's highest accolade for conspicuous bravery. I am truly indebted to these kind and considerate people who took the time and trouble to write to me offering valuable help and words of encouragement. I have to confess that not until this late stage of my life have I had any real knowledge of these brave men and their deeds. Like many of my contemporaries, I took such valour for granted. However, if this belated attempt at paying homage helps ensure a continuing interest in the lives of the recipients, or arouses or revives interest in other seemingly forgotten heroes, then my work will have been worthwhile.

There has been a temptation from time to time to compare one Victoria Cross deed with another, a temptation which I have tried to resist. In my somewhat elementary researches, I have been generally and genuinely appalled by the horrors which have been perpetrated and endured in the service of one's country. I am also conscious that the holders of the Victoria Cross are the selected representatives of many, many more very brave men and women who gave their all in their country's cause. I have no wish to demean the achievements of those who hold the Cross, but I feel certain that our heroes would never want us to forget their many colleagues who deserved to be recognised as much as or even more than they themselves, had fate or circumstance so decreed. My own active service was of little consequence – I was called up early in 1945 and spent most of my time in Italy, serving with the Royal Electrical and Mechanical Engineers until 1948.

Reading the numerous accounts of these great men, I constantly felt personally involved in the events that surrounded them: the great sacrifices made, the sweethearts, wives, children and parents whose pride was so severely tempered by poignant loss. I was also struck by the many mysteries with which some of our heroes surrounded themselves almost like a shield against the 'fame' attracted by their achievements. How sad it was that so many of them were eventually to leave this world friendless and almost forgotten.

I hope that these notes will be read with interest. I hope that my list is complete, but would not be surprised to learn that there are more Liverpool-born heroes than the 14 I have identified. We have good cause to be grateful to every one of them, for it is to them and their companions that we owe the quality of life which we presently enjoy.

The Victoria Cross

Instituted on 29 January 1856, the Victoria Cross is awarded only to those of the armed forces who merit the honour – 'For Conspicuous Bravery'. The principle has been upheld that no other circumstances, neither rank, nor length of service nor severity of wounds would be considered. Initially it was awarded retrospectively to cover the Crimean War (1854-1856) and the first 62 Victoria Crosses were presented by HM Queen Victoria in Hyde Park, London on 26 June 1857.

The Cross is described as a 'cross patée of bronze, one and a half inches in diameter', and is made from the metal of Russian guns captured at Sevastopol. In the centre is the Royal Crown surmounted by a lion and beneath is a scroll with the words 'For Valour' inscribed. The date of the act of gallantry is engraved on the reverse side and the holder's name is to be found on the reverse of the clasp. The ribbon was originally blue for the Royal Navy and red for the Army, but under a Royal Warrant of 1920 this was changed to crimson for both services.

The Victoria Cross has precedence and is worn before all other decorations and on the left breast. If the ribbon only is worn, a small replica of the Cross is fixed in the centre. The award is not given lightly for there is strict scrutiny of every recommendation. A comparison seems to show that the Cross may have been awarded more frequently before the 1914-18 War than since the end of that war – for instance, the number of Victoria Crosses awarded in the Indian Mutiny was the same as for the whole of the Second World War. It must be remembered, however, that at that time the only other award available to recognise bravery in service was the Distinguished Conduct Medal, whereas now there are ten alternative honours. It would seem that a most important criterion for the Victoria Cross is that of self-sacrifice – an act of heroism, often performed on more than one occasion, in which the individual, regardless of his own safety, attempts to rescue, protect or support his fellow men or vital equipment in the face of the enemy. It also includes acts of daring leadership to secure objectives in the face of tremendous danger and in doing so to save lives and restore faltering morale. This booklet gives examples of both.

The total number of Victoria Crosses awarded up to now stands at 1355, including one to the American Unknown Soldier. 112 were awarded in the Crimean War; 182 in the Indian Mutiny; 225 for the China Campaign, Zulu War, Sudan and South African Wars. In the Great War (1914-1920), 633 were awarded; in the inter-war years, 5; and in the Second World War, 182. Since then 4 were awarded in Korea, 1 in Sarawak, 4 to Australians in Vietnam, 2 in the Falklands Conflict of 1982 and one in Iraq.

Only three people have earned double VCs; three have been awarded to fathers and sons; and four pairs of brothers have earned the award. The youngest winners – Thomas Flynn in the Indian Mutiny and Andrew Fitzgibbon in the China War of 1860 – were both just 15 years old. The oldest recipient is believed to be William Raynor during the Indian Mutiny, who was nearly 62 years of age. Accepting that the Victoria Cross is awarded only during times of conflict, it is not surprising that there are now very few surviving holders of the award. In 1952, there were 412 surviving holders; by 1976 that number had fallen to 117; and in 1984 there were only 68, of whom only 8 remained from the 1914-18 war. There are now only 12 survivors – none from the First World War – including the most recent, Private Johnson Beharry. 8 survive from the Second World War, including Liverpool's Lt Commander Ian Fraser. The last surviving Great War recipient was Air Commodore Ferdinand M.F.West who earned his VC on 10 August 1918 in France, serving with 8 Squadron Royal Air Force and died almost 80 years later in 1998. The two Falklands War recipients, Colonel H.Jones and Sergeant I.J.McKay, received their awards posthumously.

Holders of the Victoria Cross below the rank of commissioned officer were granted pensions, initially of £10 per year with £5 for a Bar. Paltry as this sum may seem, it was to remain unchanged until 1959 when the sum was increased to £100 per year, tax free, and all ranks became eligible. In 1995, the annual pension was increased to £1300. Interestingly, in a *Daily Mirror* report on 31 January 2006 about surviving VC holders, it was noted that Tulbahadur Pun VC, a Gurkha living in Nepal, was obliged to sell his VC because of financial hardship, whilst Bhanbhagta Gurung, another Gurkha also living in Nepal, found that his £1300 annual pension made him 'one of the richest men in the region'.

In the original Royal Warrant there was an expulsion clause which would permit a recipient's name to be erased from the Register for certain discreditable conduct and thereby cancel the pension. HM King George V felt strongly that there should never be any circumstances which should make the award forfeit and although the expulsion clause still remains it is highly unlikely ever to be invoked.

In 1902, King Edward VII approved the important principle of awarding the Victoria Cross posthumously; and in 1911, King George V decreed the eligibility of native officers and men of the Indian Army. In 1920, the award was extended to include the Royal Air Force and 'matrons, sisters and nurses, serving regularly or temporarily under orders, direction or supervision of the military authorities'. The decoration has never, as yet, been awarded to a woman.

One important aspect of the award is contained in what is referred to as 'Rule 13' of the Royal Warrant of 29 January 1856:

> *It is ordained that, in the event of a gallant and daring act having been performed by a squadron, ship's company, a detached body of Seamen and Marines not under 50 in number, or by a brigade, regiment company or troop, in which the Admiral, General or other Officer Commanding such forces may deem that all are equally brave and distinguished so that no special selection can be made by them, then in such case the Admiral, General or Officer Commanding may direct that for any such body of Seamen or Marines, or for every troop or company of Soldiers, that one Officer shall be selected by the Officers engaged for the decoration. And in a like manner one Petty Officer or Non-commissioned Officer shall be selected by the Petty Officers and Non-commissioned Officers engaged and two Seamen or Private Soldiers or Marines shall be selected by the Seamen, Private Soldiers or Marines engaged respectively, for the decoration; and the names of those selected shall be transmitted by the Senior Officer in command of the Naval Force, Brigade, Regiment, Company or Troop, to the Admiral or General Officer Commanding who shall in due manner confer the decoration as if the acts were done under his own eye.*

That paragraph takes some reading but has affected the award to a number of recipients over the years (see for example Ronald Neil Stuart VC in *Liverpool Heroes* Book I.).

* * * * *

In May 2009, the surviving Victoria Cross holders were as follows:

Tulbahadur Pun, 6th Gurkha Rifles, June 1944 in Burma. Now 85 years of age.

John Cruickshank, Royal Air Force Volunteer Reserve, July 1944 over the Atlantic. Now 88 years of age.

Lachhiman Gurung, 8th Gurkha Rifles, May 1945 in Burma. Now 91 years of age.

Ted Kenna, Australian Imperial Force, May 1945 in New Guinea. Now aged 86 years.

Bill Speakman, Black Watch, November 1951 in Korea. Now 81 years of age.

Rambahadur Limbu, 2nd Battalion, 10th Princess Mary's Own Gurkha Rifles, November 1965 in Borneo. Now 69 years old.

Keith Payne, 1st Battalion Royal Australian Regiment, May 1969, in Vietnam. Now 75 years old.

Johnson Beharry, Princess of Wales's Royal Regiment, May 2004 in Iraq. Now 29 years old.

Willie Apiata, New Zealand Special Air Service, Afghanistan 2004. Now 36 years old.

Mark Gregor Donaldson, Australian Special Air Service, Afghanistan September 2008. Now 30 years old.

APPENDIX II

The Memorial

The Memorial to Noel Chavasse, VC and Bar, an adopted son of Liverpool, and 15 other recipients of the Victoria Cross who were born in Liverpool, is the brainchild of local Chavasse admirers. They met in July 2005 and declared their intention of securing a fitting memorial. Ambitious? Optimistic? Foolhardy? My answer to each would have to be 'Yes!' – but the group's determination to succeed has never wavered.

Members of the NCVCMA Committee at the Memorial in Abercromby Square,
Liverpool, August 2008

The sculptor is a local man, Tom Murphy, who has a long history of producing memorable pieces in Liverpool. He is responsible for the Shankly statue at Liverpool Football Club, the John Lennon statue at our airport, the Moores Brothers statue formerly in Church Street but now in Old Hall Street, the Captain Johnny Walker statue at the Pier Head, the Blitz Memorial at Liverpool Parish Church, and many others. It seemed logical to us that Tom should be our man, especially as we knew he shared our admiration for Chavasse and our other 'Liverpool Heroes'. We consulted the Chavasse family and the Regimental Associations and all agreed that we should aim for a traditional bronze work which would strive to show the character and personality of Noel Chavasse, rather than a particular moment in history. We also agreed that both the Royal Army Medical Corps and the Liverpool Scottish allegiances of Chavasse should feature, together with one of his stretcher-bearers - Noel was always anxious to remind people of their bravery. Within these parameters, Tom's design has found favour not only with us but also with the family and military, and I leave it to him to describe our memorial.

Bill Sergeant, Chairman, NCVCMA

Design of the NCVCMA Memorial

It was decided almost from the outset that the Chavasse sculpture celebrating the heroic deeds of Captain Noel Chavasse could not be depicted using a single figure. He was not a glory seeker; his deeds arose from his dedication as a doctor, a real professional and above all a committed Christian. He would not have been comfortable with a statue which did not pay tribute to a brave stretcher-bearer. A wounded soldier became the third figure.

A three-figure grouping provided an ideal opportunity for an action sculpture, and a work which is meant to be interesting from all viewing angles. The sculptural group forms an offset triangle, or a wave set on a slight gradient. The angular lines throughout the piece create an impression of forward propulsion and a sense of struggle. In line with the conditions of the time, the figures look as if they are on an endless challenging journey.

The figures are displayed on an oblong base reminiscent of the Cenotaph, and the sloped sides of the base include tributes to 15 Liverpool-born Victoria Cross winners. Captain Chavasse is portrayed straining under the weight of the wounded soldier, whose whole body and arms are extended across the length of the sculpture in a cruciform shape.

The sculpture has many fine details: Chavasse himself is depicted wearing the Liverpool Scottish Glengarry with his RAMC uniform – perhaps not strictly accurate in the context of battle but symbolic of his everlasting affection for the Liverpool Battalion. He supports a wounded soldier by stretching his right arm over his shoulder and clasping the

wrist of the wounded man. At the same time, he supports the wounded man's upper torso with his other arm. The powerful stretcher-bearer at the rear contorts his body to assist in the lift, and his concern for the wounded man's obvious ankle injury is apparent. In this kneeling position, the famous Liverpool Scottish kilt is clearly displayed. The close contact of the figures, which almost seem to be welded together, echoes the compassion and camaraderie of soldiers.

The design sets out to maintain the viewer's interest throughout with the dramatic positions of the figures set at differing heights, and the mass of detail, including the way the hands are depicted - some coupled together and others stretched out dramatically - and the detail of the badges and uniforms of the RAMC, the King's Liverpool Regiment and the Liverpool Scottish.

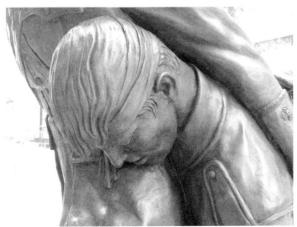

I have deliberately omitted any reference to the weapons of war as this sculpture is primarily about the triumph of love and compassion in laying down one's life for another. This message will be as relevant for generations to come as it was in 1914-18. It is important to emphasise that although this memorial depicts Noel Chavasse, it nevertheless commemorates the valour and deeds of fifteen other recipients of the Victoria Cross, several of whom, like Chavasse, lost their lives whilst helping their fellow men. Chavasse epitomises the bravery of all such men to whom this memorial is a lasting tribute.

I am proud to have been chosen for this Commission. My words do it scant justice for, after all, this sculpture is meant to be seen.

Tom Murphy, Sculptor